THE POET RECLINING

'The Poet Reclining' by Marc Chagall (1915)

KEN SMITH

The Poet Reclining

SELECTED POEMS 1962-1980

BLOODAXE BOOKS

ISBN: 0 906427 50 9 hardback
       0 906427 51 7 paperback

First published 1982 by
Bloodaxe Books Ltd,
P.O. Box 1SN,
Newcastle upon Tyne NE99 1SN.

The publisher acknowledges the financial assistance
of Northern Arts.

Typesetting & cover printing by
Tyneside Free Press Workshop Ltd, Newcastle upon Tyne.

Printed in Great Britain by
Unwin Brothers Ltd, Old Woking, Surrey.

This book is for Judi

Acknowledgements

This selection includes poems from thirteen books and pamphlets published in Britain and America. Full details are given in the bibliography (pages 199-201).

Ken Smith wishes to thank the Arts Council of Great Britain for a Writer's Bursary awarded in 1975. Some poems from *The Pity* formed part of a collection which won an Eric Gregory Award in 1964.

The frontispiece is a black and white reproduction of the painting 'The Poet Reclining' by Marc Chagall (Tate Gallery, London) © A.D.A.G.P. Paris, 1982.

Contents

The Eli Poems

THE POET RECLINING

Family Group

He also was a stormy day: a squat mountain man
smelling of sheep and the high pasture, stumping
through pinewoods, hunched and small, feeling
the weather on him. Work angled him.
Fingers were crooked with frost, stiffened.

Ploughing he would fix his eye on the hawthorn,
walking firm-booted, concerned for the furrow.
Horse and man in motion together, deliberate,
one foot put before the other, treading cut clay.
He would not see the bird perched on the plough.
He would not chase the plover limping over stubble.

He was my father who brought in wood and lit
the hissing lamp. And he would sit, quiet
as moor before the fire. She drew him
slowly out of silence. She had a coat
made from a blanket and wore boys' shoes.
She was small and had red hands, firm-boned,
and her hair was greying. The house was stone
and slate. It was her house, his home,
and their family, and they quarrelled often.

She churned butter, baked, and scrubbed floors,
and for forty years he laboured the raw earth
and rough weather. In winter we made mats
from rags with pegs. We guarded ourselves
and were close. We were poor and poorer banking
each pound saved. Each year passed slowly.

Now he lives in the glass world of his shop,
and time is grudged. Ham and tinned meat
and vegetables are his breathing day.
He works harder and is unhappy. She too
stoops through the labouring year, is greyer
and grumbles. Nothing gets made any more
but money that cannot be made. Nothing
means happiness. The light comes down wires,
water through tubes. All is expensive, paid.

Silence is gone from their lives, the city
has taken that poised energy. Violence
is articulate. The deliberate motion is gone
and he moves with pain through time that is work
that is cash. He will not notice the crashed
gull fallen in the storm, the grabbing sparrows.
She cannot ease him into speech, or be content
before the broody fire. She is in fashion now.
But seasons pass them without touching.
They will not feel the winter when it comes.

The street

leads nowhere, cannot be entered,
down which no one is walking

into the silence, the pure sea
of boats, cryings, scuffed quays.

The grey air is empty, built into
cloud-columns. Street of childhood,
        no one is calling.
In its doorways no person is standing
nor stares from one house to another.

        Things happen to us.
War boarded these windows, split walls
spilled in the held spaces.

In the growing dark only a sadness
presses the stairs to the stilled rooms

whose walls peel like maps. Here the guns
and the toys become one another. The war

has moved off. Who left can't return.
Who lived here forgot the clear lines

the far buildings had, *it has happened*
we say, the sound bobs on the water.

Who stares at the great shadows, remembers
a voice, forgets whose, who watches

the sunlight fall, there, between high houses
themselves fallen, his feet don't lead back.

Who had a house now has a stone.

Country: Keld to Reeth

Each day the earth offers itself
to the sun's heat, water.

A picture I carry, a country
all weeds, pale flowers
shaped in poor soil.
The rain drifts over it, I hear
my feet crush the winter grass,
see my father who walks in a landscape
that seems not growing but shrinkage.

Returning, he did not pause on the hill
between the still faces of horses.

We were a darker blur on the stubble,
a fragment in time gone, we left
not a mark, not a footprint;
the cold forest, the birds of the moor
do not recall us.

The hills lie on anvils of stone,
sheepcut, shaped by all weathers.
Great stones squat on the ridges
as if the ice might come back for them.
A few harebells lift to the wind.
There is a ragged field, patches of bramble.

Grass

Grass erupts slowly, locking the soil in frail roots.
Without these tenoned fingers earth would be as sea,
drifting, unsure. It is a sort of knowledge,
gripping together, confirming that hill's shape.

Do not forget the grass. That trodden softness
could only be an innocence that insists, comes back,
season by growing season. It cannot stop itself.
And though you kill it, grass does not seem to die.

Rocks morticed in themselves do not require it,
nor does its colour clutch the spaces of the desert.
Its absence is death's sign, brooding its own mystery.
Grass exists. All life revolves around its rooted blade.

And yet grass does not care. Accepting without flower,
it seeds on plains or in cracked rocks, indifferent
to a touch that sears the granite. Grass
moves on, impotent in will, a rooted apathy
exposed to hoof and fire. It cannot stop itself.
Grass waits the mower's knife, the ditcher's spade.

The pity

> *'I cut my hands on the cords at the strangling post*
> *but no blood spilled from my veins;*
> *instead of blood I watched and saw the pity run out of me'*
> – Mao Tse-tung

She was destroyed and my child ceased in her belly.
In Kiang-si we had walked in the clear morning,
she hanging back, barefoot, childbig. Crossing
the plank bridge I saw the falling mountain
with its stream hang still. The land lay like a bowl
of pebbles, hills behind me at its rim. A hawk
splayed in the wind, dived to kill; so sparrows die.
China was patience you said: the sketched lines
of valley and the reaching twig, all still, rest in motion;

a large pale flower twitching, a flower waiting, open.
So a vast land itched for death, its people mild
and ministered.
                    But the cockroach and the grinning toad
drawn beautiful was China; the fly grown fat on flesh,
glittering in heat. I was lashed and drained
of the gentle passion. Patience was prised from me.
I picked lice from my hair. You thought me gentle still.
I ate filth, wore it, would have died in filth.

The horned and hanging bat sees a bat's world.
Fish quiver in the shallows, cold as their element,
thinking water. I wore contempt, grew hatred.
I was locked and jailed. She that was my wife
was garrotted. And compassion had not anything to do
with this; she was destroyed where I could hear,
and the child ceased in her.

Compassion cannot go forever in the sun,
paraded, bowing, twig-like. It rests,
and somewhere takes the hawk's wing, diving.

She was destroyed and my child ceased.
I cut my hands on the cords at the strangling post,
but no blood spilled from my veins;
instead of blood I watched and saw the pity run out of me.

The hunter

On the hill three hawks
on spread feathers
fish the summer grass.

In summer on the bare hill
the light falls in sheets.

The sheep turn like ships
at their moorings.

The crows fly downwind,
their sounds fall from the sky,
downwind they are crying.

Man, dog, birds. On the hill
sheep and the wrenched grass
lie downwind. It is summer.

The birds crossing the sky
are naked, the light falls,
downwind they are falling.

It is summer,
dog and man share the hill,
sniff the air,
hunt the birds.

As we look in the tunnel
for the end
for the bleak
unblinking eye of the daylight

he is looking
for the black holes in the sky.

Water

1

a country beginning to open its spaces
a silence being broken by voices

over the first wrecked cliffs
darknesses moving in darkness

the sea keeps moving up. The sea
comes with a thin razor of water

it takes what it gives
the salt white birds fly over it

the sea wipes off the footprints of gulls
this country seems grass under the feet

its sounds are not shaken like trees
its shapes do not move like slow horses

no metal rings through this silence

in half-light the coasts lift themselves
a sea beats on them, is wild to come in

2

the cold of the wind is not from the sea
not absence of sun makes this darkness

in the dry river-bed I have seen
even the granite rippled by water

the rocks lie without ease on each other
hills scoured by rainfall wait for the sea

the sea holds a knife to the land, breaks
out the first stone shells. The sea

takes the land away, moans, lifting small
white flags in this impossible darkness

A fragment

out of our joined
lives is grey sky
mountain and pine
grey lake, late summer
the year of our child.

For you there were faces
snarled in your coatsleeve,
you were a creature trapped

in its flesh, in its pain
the roots of your hair
the knife of my body
the night, the light
hurt you, the light
streamed out of you.

Under the wood the child
opened its mouth
to the earth of your breasts.

We became under the rain
the mountain the reeds
one cry, smaller than a minute
three mouthed
a small shrill crying.

* * *

The stone poems

1

A man's work
he must bend for them,
his lifting become
stone-shut
with a stone's presence.

Stone of house, stone
of monument.
Nothing in their gift.

Stone in a man's field
or a man's shoe –
piece of the Earth's
wish to be idle, rid of us,
fraction of misery.

Not as the sea is:
weeds, birdcries, a fish
glancing the sunk light.

Sea changes totally,
stone rarely. The dead
form a new kind of stone.

It will not alter. Snap
and be nattered to dust
or the chafing of water.

Part of the sea asleep
in its own shadow. Part
of its stone.

2

Either he shifts it
or goes round it.

Dragged to the field's edge
to be grown over, useful there.

Others rise in the rain,
chiselled by frost,
tossed up by boys.

Some arrive strangely by night
or happen as comets do. In New England
frost forces them out,
stone on the move.

And some lie continually
in the field's road
finding their ways back
into bleak malevolent creatures
wanting to sit in open fields.

The man keeps pelting them
in a backward whirlpool of stones
slewed over centuries.

As if this were a battle: a man
hurling stones and the stones'
slow returns to their orbits.

As if they would lie barearse
to the sun, giving nothing growth.

3

Stonecold we say. The great music
goes on without them,
Mozart's mind forming again
in the members of the orchestra,
in the air, in the bow
touching the string, the conductor
commanding what he heard once
of rivers, of stones, birds, men.

In the blank faceless thing
nothing of our meanings
but that it outlasts us, holds up
the names that mean nothing now
in the wind wearing them away
where the scripts change
and the dialects weather
as the words shift their meanings
in the long war with silence
till what's left is a finger-traced
blur where the chisel cut
let vandals look upon this epitaph.

That it is stone, that
it is cold, that it is
chosen for sepulchres.

Nothing there: a few bones
picked clean as sticks
and the seasons drained out:

a stone flag,
a lament for dead people.

And nothing in that, nothing
can be staved off: mine
is a stoney vision they say.

Out in the strange light
grown in the world.

4

Absence of stone
assenza di pietre,
the stone
solo pietra raschiata
scraped to its usefulness.

Stone taken into speech,
stone touched in a bargain,

counting stone, stone
turning in the mill,
the ruminant, *la ruminante*.

Stone taken from the moon,
I have since touched one.

Stone ballast used again
building the shipman's house,
the miller's table.

A Roman stone I took
years ago that had lain
centuries its pavement
under the Saxon graveyard.

Stone of absence
pietra di assenze.
Stone of Beethoven's fist.

No more the miracle of gneiss,
nor graining nor quartz,
no scourings of rivers,
no granite, no dross
nor the eye of volcano
né l'occhio dei vulcani,
so little, the hot gas
of atoms blown back into space
that were Socrates, chert,
flakes of flint tool,
touch of all lovers, *di fiumi
massi, puddinghe, detriti.*

Nothing grown wild,
moving strangely, not moving
till the long ice moves them.

Not the bull's dark,
l'oscurita del toro.
Not the beasts' wonder,
*la meraviglia delle bestie
stupite della loro stessa nascita*

over their own birth.

Not lichened over
under half the stars.

Not city stone nor stone
the wind forgot.

No stone at all:
a land gleaned clean.

5

All through stone. Things
immersed in it
become stone.

Without feature or interest
to what ice or water
scrapes it to.

Anonymous,
not dreaming nor dancing.

Intending nothing –
neither the good house
nor arrowhead
nor inconvenience.

Resisting.
Not resisting.
Holding on while the planet
shudders into more stones.

Nothing to be done
but be a grey boulder
or be pebble or be sand.

No inside, no outside, no centre.
No squatting like an animal.
No nesting like a bird.

Not wanting to go back
into rock, not wanting
to enter the sea, not wanting
to be a small red flower
or a black shoe
or a lost button.

Not likeable.

Not bothered.

6

Turned in the hand, idly,
to the contempt of the busy.

What it would be
to be brought to it
forever in its place.

A man's say to be
pig figure, bird entering flight
or the tiny house of a snail,
replica of the southern wind.

A man's say. Not a thing
to do with all he says of it,
no more than birds their names.

That it may look
from the church wall
a man sharpens chisels.

From the bleak glance
of quarries came footstools,
thrones, the gargoyle's
snarling waterspout,
knights in stone armour,
the poor kneeling or stooping,
stone thumb to the stone nose
in contempt of their masters,

locked beasts, Siva's dance,
a man peering so long
till the seawind wears him away.

The man's tools seek
a stone anaconda.

Bunched in riverbeds,
abandoned, stones
lie down anywhere.

They will not answer
out of the strange mouth
of the dead.

They will never mean anything.

Their silence
applauds them.

* * *

Exiles
(for Marek Laczynski)

One the foreign woman

More than my life's map
of notebooks and lost gloves
I know the moon's other look.

I remember a hat rolling
and rolling. No name
no other detail swings
in that street's wind.

Counting the steps to my room
in the damp house I glimpse
the fence and the roof
of my grandfather's house.

Here I continually
open a drawer on the dust
trapped under newspaper.

I look through the glass
at an indifferent skyline.
I count the steps
in a strange house.

Two the return

Objects, clenched in their
separateness. Streetnames,
a park, the Jewish memorial.

In a place changed
out of my presence I find
known friends in strangers.

I remember I say, being
deceived, touching
the stopped door to a room
lit with child's songs.

Dead streets, dead houses,
dead people. Here I walk
with my eyes turned away
not to see absences, blind windows.

Three the photograph

Face of Kafka, the camera
flattened old shadows that moved
in the eyes and mouthcorners.

How much of our lives is filed
in deep drawers, a red form
for my birth, a black for my death.

Documents, passports, the
European darkness is trapped
in the breath of officials –
jobs to do, quotas to fill.

As we learned when the shoes
were fetched up and counted
and the long graves were dug.

Out of that darkness ashes
and letters and photographs.

Stopped in a fragment
the shutter admitted
the curious look of a man.

The smile and the angle
of sunlight survive him.

Dream journeys

In the last light we made camp.
I slept with the dogs' whimpering
and dreamed of the continent, a fierce mask.
From doorways the people offered their indifference
or crept through the bush to watch us. One came,
bent and crow-faced from years listening
to the desert. I recall he was dumb
and told off the words on the palm of the woman
who spoke for him. No more of that place than we,
his way lay south as ours west by the mountain.
I knew roads to the places he spoke of.
By the fire a stranger, in the dream
I knew him far back. His was old news
of burnings and wanderings, of the people
who spread through these lands.
I half-slept, the men with us listening
for some wonder. When she described the sea
our people opened their mouths, though I had once
seen it myself, grey and endless, like our way.
I was kept silent, it was nothing.
In that woman's voice I fell into deep sleep,
all the ages of Europe elaborated,
a mathematics of blood. At the last
he walked between land and sea, a man
centuries old stepping the waterline stones
with an easy care, his eye never to one side
but to the edge of water and haze, and stepping so
a child came whom he seized and ate,
throwing aside what was half-eaten
as he came to the distance, without pause.

She speaks

This late evening, years
it seems, years I have been sitting,
the life in me sleeping, the chair
grown to me, drawing

round me the figure of my quiet. In which
I have sat out his silences, silences
in stone and coral, silences beyond sleep
and still water. Not him I endured
but his speechlessness –
wanting him cupped to my ear,
him shape to my sounds, years
not knowing what name rode in his skull,
what cry might break at the end of it.
Night after night, till he rises,
winding the clock, dropping his boots,
turning toward me as if he contained
other lives, as if
he were the sum of all the dead trying to get out.

Years of this. Grumbling asleep
names from a sunk continent, strange words
with salt and age in them. Or I have caught him
alone on a street saying aloud
A man lives when his name is pronounced.

Whose name? who lives? I ask
the slope of his shoulder, his shut jaw.
Or will he never speak again? I don't know
how to open him, how to enter
this difference, this mountain of quiet,
chipping it, savouring moments of speech
when he plays family man and looks up
over the offering bowls of his table
to where I have my own name ready to be spoken,
and the child's tricks, and things he must buy.
I offer tiny stones from my own house.
That he hates. He thinks he is heather
taken from the moor, continually bent
to a wind no longer pressing it, he's like a stone
shaped by water water shall not have again.

Am I to wait at the mouth of this man
the dead lunge through? I don't know what beasts
stalk me, what dancing goes on in his head.
I watch, letting him see that I watch,
catching his postures to the bathroom mirror,

talking to himself.
There'll be no steps I can't dance.
And I can't sing there'll be no song.
I'm his cynic, his lame mule,
I clatter my pans in his ear.
I shall blow his house down.
I am anti-matter, he shall be my omega.

Go teach the birds singing.
Go talk with the dead.
Go walk in the graveyard.

The child's version

Twaddle her mouth said, tired
that she knew better, given up
to the mouth's part.

In his notebook
the air takes the smell and shape
of rooms of unfinished things –
clock parts, bits to set moving,
queerly shaped pebbles.

Little use to a people hoping
one day to jump on the moon's face.
I should not put a frame to him.
Imagine him water, taking any shape
while the shape is, untrustworthy.

Everything discarded: wood and stone
he chipped to unreconciled faces,
obsessions with maps, codes, mirrors,
or wondering how it would be
to have never seen horses.

They were ashamed of their own sounds,
I know that she bore me in terror
less of pain than of pain's cry.

I am a leaf at its edge, turning
its growth back, fashioning
the image of his face in sunlight.

She is pictured turning away.
Mostly I see him staring
into a field of yellow flowers,
staring and nodding gravely
with the worldless dignity
of big flowers, curious, unyielding,
part of that tall yellow dancing.

The boss

The stone of his life weighs on him.
My life's work My life's work he whispers
holding the stone, his hands open.

It lies on us. House-stone, stone
of his past, his years are the one stone
soothed to his shape our lives lie under.

There are other stones: his wife and her two stone breasts,
his money, his speechless look through the window,
his children, carrying their own lives.

His ambition is the great stone he carries.
We polish the stone, it is our lives are worn.

We polish the stone, his house rears in the suburbs.
We polish the stone, he dreams and fears loneliness.
We polish the stone, he grows famous.

His is the stone on us when we are still.
His is the stone announcing itself when we move.
Our lives tremble, we cry *the stone the stone.*

The son

He inhabits corners of their lives,
his cry forever raised in them.
He is running into the yard or the sea.
His voice deepens, there is mud on his clothes,
tar on his boots, it happens continuously.
He goes into the army, he comes back and marries.
He lives far away, he still eats with them.

Wherever he is now he is the same
staring at nothing or holding still
for the camera. The son who dreams
looks from all the photographs, he hides
in the cupboard with old shoes.

The son who went off one day.
The son who has wife and children.
The son who works out of town.
The son who is in another country,
where it rains the same rain.

He's in the house they made,
he uses the furniture and spoons in the drawer.
He's in with the paint, always around
with the dust, he stares through the window,
he's expected any moment, food is waiting.

Forever leaping through air, or waving,
or asleep in the shed.
His look is familiar. He is the son.
When he comes back he wonders where he is,
when they speak of him he wonders
who they are speaking of.

Everything is ready.
He wipes off his plate.
Now he wants none of it.

Gravedigger

Before him go the armies, the metals shining.
Up the green hill
go the hobbling women spitting smoke,
the processions of sadly missed wives.

So much spent muscle and bullet.
So many stopped quarrels.
The shoemaker but sleeps.
The bird sings in the high trees.
There is a silence of wheat.

Who owns the dead who are always dead –
men once trees in their own land,
women desirable as water?

He spits on his hands grey with earth.

He rules with a shovel.

His spade speaks for him.

Bitter

This is the house, good as a shoe.
One by one
the dead years count themselves.

The words are old, the mouth
just goes round them.
She sings for the wrecked moon.

For love the miracle of touch.
All the miles go underfoot.
Too many trains, too many neons.

She sings for the coloured lights.
She is singing the one word *bitter*.

Grown with water in the cracks,
bitten into the roots of stones.

It wants to make everything dust.

Where winter begins

Birds fly south, a saw
yells through the woods.
Night is coming, water
chirrs in the stream.

I want to be an animal
between one sound
and another. At evening
I come to a river, the reeds
like the dark in my own skull.
I want to sleep, to be still
away from the villages,
night is coming.

Image of bird in the sky,
image of leaf, shadow on shadow.
Darkness begins in the trees
and the tight maize-heads.

Burrowed out of the owl's look
I dream the shush of grass
in the night fields, sleeping.

In Pennsylvania, winter's end

A year I turned in myself
like a sail, round and around
turning to voices
caught by the light.

The dancers are turning
to look, asking who partners them,
poised as they move they see
how the light moves on itself.

I lay on the side of a hill
in summer, the hill
that is as the side of my own life.
The grasses rippled, ancient.

I became very small
and entered my body, seeing within
dancers crossing the slope far away.

Are they arriving or leaving?
Are theirs these voices calling
back or beyond them?

Under the hill an iron bell
rocked by the moon is booming,
its sound a slow tide,
wells of sweet water.

After a journey

When we wake
snow will lie on the sills. There are things
happening when no one knows it.

I returned from the west finding the trees bare.
With the first cold my children came,
I don't know where they learn their songs from.

I know the dead have little to say to us,
but speak like they were the same, like clocks
scuttling into the dark with the same nothings.

Later perhaps they turn aside to a place
where they no longer need us to listen, or go out
when they are at peace like burned wicks.

What we don't know yet is no matter.
I pray not to a god but to stone,
to the grass, to the running hooves of the horses.

Little notes

Nick draws her brother.
In the enormous eyes
are pictures
of people and flowers.

This wood then, its grain
recorded itself growing.
And these stones of the cathedral,
what do they record?

Oh the small agonies,
men and women in time –
dancing, dancing, bread
and a short life.

The moon's a round cry.
Take a good look
before it's covered in moss.
Nick says the moon is the moon.

She draws her mother,
one breast then the other.
Draw me the sounds
of her feet, of her breathing.

Persistent narrative

The speaker opens his mouth.
The lovers lie down together.
The boy is sent to the war.

The last train leaves the city.
The sky clouds over with ruin.
The animals step back into shadow.

The speaker opens his mouth.
The fields are trampled by horses.
Children crouch in the ashes.

Survivors wait at the frontier.
Two armies meet in a forest.
The lovers take off their clothes.

The speaker opens his mouth.
An earthquake topples the belltower.
The boy lies down in a cornfield.

Soldiers patrol all the streets.
The grocer has run out of flour.
The girl dreams of a wheatfield.

The speaker opens his mouth.
Now the woman sweeps out her house.
Now there is a christening.

The ship enters the harbour.
The girl waves her red scarf.
The lovers cry out in their love.

And at last it is still.
And the speaker says *I shall begin.*
The children are all asleep.

Crying woman

She is making her sounds, the ones for everyone else.
She goes *cri-cri* like a walking bird and then
sounds of a big bird alert on the rocks.
Crying woman makes the sound of a baby about to be fed.
This one is the sound of someone alone a long time,
the sound of someone cast out at sea, the sounds

of wreckers guiding a boat to their reef,
of the ship's crew who are drowning
and the indignations of those who tell this years after.
This one is from the mountains, she makes big sounds
full of cloud and rain, she begins her infinity.
This one cries *mother*, thinking of her people.
When she thinks of the south she sings
like someone asleep in the sun all day.
This one the otter. This one the gazelle
running for love of running. And this one
who is quiet a long time is a gull
pitching out from the cliff between land and sea
till she becomes the air she swings on. This one
begins shouting straight off and never stops,
a devourer that wants everything at once.
This one is creeping through grasses to ambush,
and at last she's a spilled song
finishing somewhere into the roofbeams.
Silence is hers, she makes that
when she thinks of another, when through her sleep
her children are running too near the water.
The cry of an animal kicked awake to its guard,
noises of something lost in the thicket, she croons
the names of old lovers dead in the wars.
Some sounds come from nowhere, she wants
a man who lives on the moon's back, she wants
to die if she does for eternity what she does now.
The first awake in the camp, she's about
seeking warmth, she goes out of her self's house.
She's the first creature to crawl out of the sea.
She makes all sounds, I don't know if she's one or many.
If ever she puts them together at once I shall drown
and drift with her in the sea off Northumberland
crying *forever forever*, awake to the last star.

Song for the whites

I live away from my own people among strangers
for whom words have too many shadows.
Back there my mouth turned to a taste of ashes.

I sit all night writing my songs
for no instrument that no throat sings,
and don't care if they're bad, to be tied up
with strings like a doctor's skeleton.

Most days I make small voices. Sometimes at night
sounds run through my head that I must get up;
if the world is running to death I shall take
at least my own sounds with me. I've grown used
to the strangers, their speech no longer alien
and I see they have no covering against winds.
Come under the song strangers, I shall tell you
what you don't know and don't care for –
how when we tortured it was to respect you.
Over the best fighter we put a buffalo robe,
cut a cross in the breast of the bravest dead.
We honoured those who destroyed us.
Let me tell you about the frozen grasslands
and how when we had nothing to eat
your words were *let them eat grass*.
Let me tell you about the Cheyenne who died at Sand Creek
and of White Antelope who sang *nothing lives long*
only the earth and mountains.
You may write that in books if you will.
It was his death-song, his and the buffalo's.

From the Nahua

Down from Ometeotl who is
all pairs beyond flesh &
divisions, descending
the twelve flights through
many gods, strifes, nights,
the birds & the sun,
the Milky Way that is
as a woman's skeleton we come
to the world we know at rest
on the backs of 4 crocodiles
supporting the 4 created

corners & floating on a lake
where are our stones & flesh

the soul travels down nine
more, passing a yellow dog
guarding the river, through
peaks to a mountain of pure
obsidian, met in turn
by bone cutting winds, flags,
arrows & wild beast, through
a narrow place to the final
rung: the ranks of the known
& the unknown. And all this
apart from the 3 heavens –
the sensual in Water & Mist,
the mind's Land of the Fleshless,
the Sun's House of Pure
Imagining, & last Mictlán
the inferno at Earth's core –
all this in time a calendar
worked from the stones
but precise as it matters,
and all a continuum bent
on itself where the soul
travels away through the flesh,
a circle begins as it ends
for those who cannot give up.

Consider this system, cut
into bloody cakes by the
Mexica, Dog People of Atlán.
And consider Hernán Cortés
arrived the appointed year
from the east, the way
of the people after the sun
to the seed ground, who
considered them *far from
the knowledge of God not
possessed of reason,*
dispensing glass beads
of syphilis & abrupter more
casual deaths in the real.

The Sioux cleared from Minnesota

I prefer women with flesh, the bones
have too much to say about cemeteries.
Here they're so thin I can't see them.

When I first came here I grew plants
that were dead by morning.
I went alone seeking quiet.

Then the subway burst through my sleep, inches away.
I prayed to whatever god listened,
hearing 15 million buffalo die.

Now when I close my eyes to talk
to the voices I hear Little Crow –
Hawk that Hunts Walking, speak out.

How he led without hope to the slaughter.
He's gone saying his people can't win,
he wants peace, not the life of a no one.

A year later shot down
picking berries, they threw him
in the offal pit. So much for Little Crow.

I've seen their cities.
I have nothing to put out but this hand
and this little glass.

Ghost songs

1
Only a little way the dead come with us
wanting to live in their names spoken out.

2
The wind follows its footprints.
I sleep in the owl's coveting watch.

3
This is the feel of belonging to no place:
the gods come loose from their stones.

4
No man can drink all of the water.
Think of the ice frozen a thousand years.

5
When the butcher comes give him bones.
When the clerk comes give him nothing at all.

6
When I draw you why do you pose so
unless I am taking something away?

7
All the facts are breaking apart.
The jetplanes are sowing dead grass.

8
If the dance takes an age I shall dance,
if my sleep lasts a minute.

9
Write it all down, enough for a postcard.
Pick someone at random and send it.

10
Send it away from you. Let them burn it.
Let them feed it to cattle.

Ghost dances

1
Whoever you are looking in I'm in here
looking out. Do you hear singing?

2
I want to be nothing more than the spaces
between sounds, as the air is between grass.

3
Once I was a road where everyone passed.
When I heard the dance first it was over me.

4
First I became dancer, then dance.
I shall fill all the room's crevices.

5
For music I need my hands and my feet.
Let the rest of me join and fill like a smoke.

6
Let the air be the crows', to the fish water.
My sign is an ear of good wheat.

7
The animals come and go. The sea
doesn't go down forever.

8
The automobile is a dead beast going the way
of the mammoth. Let it go.

9
I shall dance through your landscape
back to my beginnings, a thousand years.

10
We are alone here with the stones.
Dance joyfully for that woman spinning.

Where did I learn such quiet

Where did I learn such quiet, after the Punic wars
and the killing of those who surrendered,
where did I learn it?

Even Europe has come and gone and the star patterns
altered, Hannibal would no longer know
the way through the mountains. From where
did the silence come over the Polish Corridor
and the sleeping Xanthoi sentries?

Brothers the field longs again for its grass,
the wind travels the old passes, the snow begins.

* * *

THE WILD TURKEY

Wild Turkey One

All day walking, noticed
nothing unusual, nothing
that came to me: grey wind,
insect glitterings. Came
to the moor edge, trackless,
dull, too many years dying.
The hand released what it held,
what those imagings meant.
It was the first time, a speck
of wing came away, that merely,
the dog licked my fingers,
the robin that's bird of death
in my own country stared at me.
The event would not shape itself
as a stream's name begins
from meandering waters.

A slight wind pulls at the cloth.
On the table a dead fly,
a water-drop, claim me minutely.
I am a small x in some place
I've begun to exist in.

The rain,
fills the pasture.
I listened as one who reaches
into a dream he cannot remember,
found nothing but edges, places
that quickly forget themselves,
words that aren't true.

Wild Turkey Two

A language of afterthoughts
pursuing the moment, events
swallowed in ritual.

These obeisances, rituals,
proper marks, our prescribing
objects and forms of piety, as –
let us worship the prophet's
shoebox, his glove-shadow:
all so many farewells.

And keep moving. Otherwise
the moment is vacant and free,
evading us. Lately I found
reaches of time, open lands
to be crossed in the long step
between one and the next moment.

The forests gather themselves
never to be cut there
between eyelash and eyelash.
I grow roots in myself
that I am any place, rooted
and moving, anywhere.
Soon may I learn
a language to speak to myself.

Living in the Danelaw

Hills around. That's
one picture. Also
a sense of the sea near
beyond the next town,
behind the seawind
on the bushes by the Thirsk road
twisting home. Farms
back of trees, dutch barn,

line of poplars. Far off
on one hillside a badge –
the white horse cut in lime.
Beneath that a village,
the horse in its keeping.

Here the linked consistencies,
seeds, soil, sufficient water,
blades of common grass, thistles
lording it over the field,
bird with his message of wheatstraw,
cloud shadows moving quickly
across Northumbria.
The plain of York. In and
through which my father turns,
his forearms veined, sweat-
and dirt-grained, persistent,
the picture never quite fades.
Through it I walk from school
three miles, hot, scuffing
the road, or it rains,
the ruts fill, the airfield
groans with its war. Through
the beetfield Canadian airmen
wave, bayonets flicking the rain.
Later out of the bush
steps the German they're hunting,
a man wanting home,
asks me the way seaward. And I
showed him to walk with the white
horse to his right side
long ago, in my picture of that place,
precise as to sky and land,
red-veined leaves of the beets,
cobbles of the market,
town, fields, uniforms. My father
spat on their stripes, those armies
crossing the yard end, turned
as often he turned saying *now it is
yours this world it is yours now.*

Another part of his childhood

To speak of the north
of my own life is bleak,
is to say I have
already said it.

I ran with the Swale,
clear mountain river,
around me, learned
in its stones. I was

its listener, that country
of turf and hill
falling into the cut
but oh slowly.

A hard grind, the soil
held back, the wheat
lay thin by the river,
storms raked the moor.

Abandoned farms, pit-shafts,
abbeys, monks' Latin
gravestones, the pines
reared in the drizzle.

In '47 shut in
with dead sheep the 4 month
snowfall pinned us.
Askrigg, Marske, the high

perched villages
of the Vikings
looked down on us.
My father, a small

gentle man I had seen
weep for a dead dog,
took a shotgun,
chased my uncle over the moor.

It was a life bound
to the land, to silence
of another kind, it was
the other place.

For the last time
I turn from it, I
set my face. It is
wherever I look,

shapes my life took:
the blown hill, the sun
close on the mountain,
the yellow weeds waving.

A description of the Lichway or corpse-road across Dartmoor

> LICH: *Old English* lic *as a suffix for -like (likely). Used as a*
> *noun, a word for form, body, corpse: the substance of a thing. Also*
> *see the Anglo-Saxon* hlinc *whose nearest synonym is ridge, hence*
> *a word for a boundary, or a path cresting a ridge, and so a word*
> *for link.*

From Babeny and Pizwell
west to Lydford 11½ miles
as the crow flies who needs
carry only his own death.

It seems not much,
by their ways a day and a half-day's
travel got the corpse
to Lydford Church, setting

the dead down again.
Hardly a tree for shade,
none for coffinwood. In rain
the moor runs like a sieve,

the brooks flood, clay pulls
to the roll of the slope.
In what boots they went
is not said, nor their curses.

By 1260 these villages
let off that passage.
The rest, scattered farms, inns,
Merripits and Bellever

trudged on, the Forest dead
on the dead's road converged
across Longaford, the Cowsic,
under Whittor and Whittaburrow.

King's land, men struggled
away from their masters,
scratching for tin, thin
scrawny cattle, a few oats

shared with the beasts
under one roof, chaff blown
in the Atlantic wind, survived
by the rain and fern.

And gone. Their hands
lifted the stone, sifted
the streams for metal. In winter
salted the dead down.

Not long back a traveller
lifted the bench lid on a corpse
floating in brine—the innkeeper
saved for spring burial.

Cut by enclosures, mines,
artillery ranges, theirs
is the dead's print, pressing
of feet through the strange land.

Wild Turkey Six

Wrote *walked into the field,*
the grasses waving, tall
pollen heads streaming the wind,
wind-river of seed, endless.

And there was nothing again
to be said matching that flow.
It is the wind's field,
then the grasses.

Walked, gathering the fall
about me, saying aloud
it is, it is. We the grass,
we shall live again.

A farewell to the city of Exeter in south-west England

Say goodbye love to this clock's
journey over its own face, turn
of these streets on their centre.

After four years of silence
I looked at my shoes, two shapes
of myself standing apart, ready to go.

While those others touch their lips
to their diplomas, let's leave without sound
in the living wind, saying *finis*

to the estuary reeds strange in the light
before rain, the ever arriving water.
Soon we shall learn there's no future.

The planet became infinitely small –
a turning stone mottled and veined,
a pebble alone, an eternity of shoes.

In the Americas, so the tale goes

A first grasp at land
suddenly found, in his way
he discovers a continent,
steps off to the prairie.
Fall comes, *the wild goose
has raised its accustomed cry.*

Winter approaches, the white zero
of afterwards, oh of boredom,
having seen it all, the sun
gone down on the world.
And too much yet to be said,
surprise land of river reeds

shaking in light, desert cries
strange and ancient, gaze
of the word for which all else
is afterthought, the mouth's
daft shape. And *where is
that lawing and that song*

I sang, crossing the mine waste:
pitted clay, runnels, weeds
dry and isolate, sun-split stones
of the slit hill, remember
this glazed land of the future
laid open and left by our going.

And if none may survive
we should speak our farewells
in this place. For this I turn
saying adieu to each leaf-sound,
finding the grass living again,
the red rose and the lily flower.

The author, a teacher of petomania, reflects on the shortcomings of his students

I undertake what I undertook
though they flounder, asleep
in the mysteries. *Truly*
they're not swans he said,
but I'll show them the water.

A language of afterthoughts
demanding the several attentions
there is. I teach stance, posture,
composure, the importance of silence
and waiting, how to forget,
how sleep, to see and not notice
the moment the mind
takes to its channel, its
leaping and threading and listening,
the business of dreams, visions,
and distant barely perceptible sounds
—how they effect
what is brought to the world's gate.
And oh they gape, tell us
how does this far off dubious
barking of dogs involve us?
Truly they lack duende,
watching with hard eyes, confess
they cannot enter the dream,
cannot see how the bowls
offer their silences, big leaves
bounce the rain in to their roots.
Describing the buds of the sycamore
coming out boxed each 4 to unfold
is to be in the other world
listening in this one.

Is to persist; everything's
yet to be learned, even the arts
and science of farts.

A journey through part of western Pennsylvania

Canvas shoes, pants,
a lone Indian walks
to New Wilmington
through Amish farmland,

green rolling, the houses
surprise each hill, white
as a smoke, blue doors
for their marriageable daughters.

We were driving some place,
two men nodded
waving their arms
from the Thirty Years War.

The wheat waved and nodded
over the bones
of the Erie, the Shawnee,
the Delaware, the Iroquois.

We drove though there is
no place to go and
the future is shut
by our shutting it.

For we ran much, filled
all the cracks, emptied
and filled the valleys
of the complex Earth.

And it's done, oh
bearded ones, girls in-a-ring,
grief-reared face travelling
nowhere, into Ohio.

* * *

THE ELI POEMS

The marsh

Evenings the crows pass
in and out the beech trees.
Perhaps it is autumn,
she walks the lowland.

The first pinch of winter –
red docken sticks, colour
running from the pasture,
weeds leaning east.

The stripped falling
face of the willows
is part of it. The land
levels down to the marsh.

A place the river
loses itself, boggy land
of overgrown water
the foot strikes into.

October swells in the beds
of reeds and tall grass.
She blows the thistledown,
puts her feet squarely

and passes the place
horse and man went down
at a gulp: bottomless pit
of bones and lost footholds.

Oh rumours go back, soldiers
and farmers mistaking
the look of firm footing –
ghosts, river vapours.

—Or birches at twilight
above fallen leaves, there
where the stones lie
on the slope as she goes.

As she leaves that place
that after will speak of her:
face peering through water
into a face, into a dark.

The third month

Oh she is
no one's,
her belly
is big.
       She
puts her hands
to touch, she
has tried to
ignore it, she says
who will help.
       It
cannot be stopped
now it's planted
he shrugs, his hands
face outward,
he says this or that
and goes.
      Well go
she says after
and you might.

Other times
what tones he took,
what ways
and she let,
she can't recall
now there's this.

Well
goes sometimes
a long time
between breakfast
and supper and
down along there
she lay down, he also,
under a bush, for
they met walking
by maybe chance
out by the water
and no they weren't
strangers, sat often
to the same table.
And not for the
last time they
lay so, and he
what was it
he said and what
matter: there's this
feeding itself
on herself, and him
walking away whose
short legs
pressing her down
whose eyes shut
and the damp grass
chilled her, he
muttered and cried
an animal sound.
            And see
where that got me
to herself
she says, as who
would she speak to
with nothing her own,
a thin
working girl,
that sort goes hungry
stopping up draughts,
goes down
with fever, galloping

consumption,
if only the poor
learn manners, and look
her skirt
can't afford to
trail the ground,
she'll work
till she's brought
to bed she yells
after him, slow
distant figure
crossing the street
to his house, *go*
and you might,
looking for brats,
here's brats,
go speak
with your wife
old man
old man
old man.

Eli's poem

I met a woman from the sea coast,
she took me aside in the bushes
and wrapped me around and said *we are alone*
as the moon up there is with just two sides.
I did what was to be done and came away with her.

Now I am with a crazy woman
who hurts herself with ashes and briars
running in the scrub. She takes blankets
and stuffs them under her skirt for a child.
She takes out the blanket and croons on it,
washes it, beats it with sticks till it cries
and tears it to pieces. Her lament
goes down the street on cut feet in the gravel.
She runs in a nightgown thinking she's the police

and charges anyone with ridiculous crimes
like wearing a hat sideways and walking wrong.
The people here know her and smile and say
yes they will come to the court to answer.
She writes everything down in her book.
In bed she's like trying to catch a hare.
She wants to sleep with me all night
till my back breaks, if I doze off
she wakes me crying for love.
I married a crazy woman for her brown hair.
At first I thought she was pregnant
but her blood runs, the doctor shakes his head at me.
I tell her your child is in the other country
and will not come here because of your frenzy.
She runs to the church crying she's evil,
the priest holds out his god's battered arms
and says *come child everyone's evil.*
I cool her with my breath, I cool her with water.
She's insatiable as the river, like winds
she has no place to go and runs
from whatever does not move. She's holding a wooden knife
and staring it down till it becomes pure menace
and I fear it myself. I sleep with her
because then I control her and know where she is,
but I don't know what runs in her.
Now she is out on the hill wailing
cutting her flesh on the stiff grass
where I go to her lamenting.

The rooming house

Dead girl what we did
was done against death,
our thrusting against
all the room's shadows.

I held your long hair
over your breasts,
under its glove of fur
your belly ran like an animal.

I put my hands to your hip-bones
that seemed like the gates
of the universe, I thought
one day to fall through forever.

And cried *do not go from me.*
I saw you walking around
in another place, in a small
picture of death.

Hearing the sounds you made
I held you against parting.
I came in to you, your dark
howled against my dark.

In the room now I breathe
for the smell of you, your thighs
wet as horses' flanks in harvest,
your heat's dumb flailing.

Dust you breathed, memory
of your throat-sound, your sweat
ingrained in my flesh,
a stained quilt, survive you.

His lament

Was it all my effort
to release you, all I knew
but to give sound to your moving,
a white to your stark face.

Words I had spoken, pulled out
and held near to myself
I released then, their twistings
ran clear as milk from a jar.

I saw as you saw, shimmer
of the rising wave mirrored
in the cornfield, a thrush bone
splayed on the air's flesh.

I had walked this way, I
had not seen the spidery roots
of the grass, leaf-vein division,
map of my own blood.

Birds combed the estuary mud,
water threading their prints.
You sang an old song, I
saw you glance through the air's web.

I touched the thin bones.
You cried out as I entered you,
a gull's yelp, breath-borne, all
the years of my life crying.

You died, so scrawny you were.
You moved out of the light though
a shape of the light still,
and you stir in my bones now.

The obsession

Months now I have lifted
your frail shell and listened.
You would not speak, you went out
the door down the street,
taking the fieldpath.

In the hood's shadow your face
is a blur I cannot remember.
I must read the slope
of your departing shoulder, it says
I have shaped you in words
that aren't true, in my dream
you move as you would not move.

You passed by, the water
looked up at you, ice-rimmed,
the marsh winter-stiffened.
On the slope where the trees begin
bird-prints had locked in hard ground
over each other. And here
you lost sight of yourself,
must come again and again
down the marshway, the dead end
of the recurring decimal.

In the wood fine snow grains
outline the pine needles.
How far it is to the hill
and the cart-rutted track.
Along there the trees thin out
where wind breaks the seedlings
and the ridge is bleakly open.
Far off the river widens to the sea,
a white mist. You must come again
to the scrubland down the side
where the brown turns to grey shale,
finding the house deserted.

Is this the place lady where pain
broke like a parting of oceans across you?
From here you have no name
but return and return to this room,
stoop over the linens, folding the sheets
and folding the sheets till there's nothing
and you but the want to be nothing
put away with them,
and the heat of you gone
as the room's warmth spends itself
on the window glass.

What was done

Push they said,
holding your limbs,

spread you apart.

So much joy they took
in the pain, the women
bore down on you.

All for men's pleasure
they said, they
looked most for a boy.

Of their own labours
they spoke, alternately
sweetened and bullied.

Turning hour after hour
the muscling wheel
rode through you.

And he saw you now
he'd think twice.
But they envied this.

Strangely they moved
in the old dance,
feeding up gossip.

They did what they must.
You suffered, love,
but to wag tongues.

At the last you saw
your own body's shafts
and the driving muscle

between them print out
its track, the child
leapt to their hands

and the wheel rolled
out of you, pushing
the small life from you.

The door

A few days before my father's death the last dream cried as I woke:

My name is Kate, I am an Irish girl
My name is Kate, I am an Irish girl

People might say the dreams were coincidences, dreams merely, indulgences perhaps, and that death's blank event drove them off at last. Over a month or two there had been about a dozen of them, almost always the same dream, or a part of it: marshland, hills one way, the tidal estuary of rising birds another. The marsh compelled attention, and the path through it that turned away up the slope and along a ridge of scrubby woods. The dream turned evening there among the briars. There was a dark quiet house, abandoned, the cold wind landward between clearings. The house lay at the track's end where the dream always ran out in a search through old drawers and cupboards of musty clothing and abandoned domesticity: but for what? Usually I saw different parts of the same landscape, entering the dream at different points on the journey she made through the marsh and up the slope along the ridge to the house, over and over. Crossing the field, walking through tall grass or wandering the marshes, she was always going away, always turned away from me. I saw only her back in a long shabby dress, her head's bulk of dark hair, a thin shoulder hunched inwards, turned towards the slope. I think she was a bit simple, a bit mad perhaps, quiet, sometimes clearly speaking a kind of song that in other times might have been taken for witchery or angelic wisdom:

She stood by the driven spring

She cried my love's
face down in the sea

People didn't bother with her. I don't know who he was. Eli. Not a workman. Pompous, a bully, middle-aged, kept a lodging-house, wife an invalid, perhaps a man who called himself a master builder for once putting up an outhouse. Kate roomed in his house, huddled with others in the dark under the slates like birds, the hired girls in their sleep dreading the dawnless yells of the knocker-up. When they were let work the mill swallowed them, sent them home limping, aching in every bone.

Two lay over the clover
Sunday afternoon

Three break bones in the mill
singing another tune

The Industrial Revolution broke across England. There were still cottagers working at home, proud of their cow and their loom and their kitchen gardens. There were still mechanics who could mould and cast and file and build before your face an engine worked from a rough sketch of an idea in your skull. But more and more the independents were going under, sending their wives and then their children to the mill, coming themselves when they could get work—for women were paid less and given work first, and children barely able to speak, they too were found useful and put to long labour. The workshop became a mill, the villages grew into muddy settlements, towns, cities. Rural communities shrank, many vanished into the fields. Driven off from their holdings and commons the country poor came to be hired for day labour and entered the lives of the towns. They were told they owned half the world, their empire branded into it two centuries deep. Dour, close, with a tight-mouthed humour, they became the industrial working class, a province of the rich.

Don't ask me how I fettle
don't askit me no longer

Burdock's good for nettle
Nettle's good for hunger

Somewhere Kate lived, a thin working girl, not of that place, without family. Eli got her pregnant, she died in childbirth. He grumbled that I contain her life within mine, and stood now in his way of her: that I was once that frail girl in the time of misery. He nattered so, when I tried to release her like a bird through the poem he must step out so she went away again, nothing to say to him, he would not leave me. What I said then was to do with his presence and her absence and my impatience. I was no go-between. The dreams continued, the landscape of marsh and ridge, the clear light on the reeds, opened like an eye. Small stirrings, sometimes her face in shadow, turning away—but her face, a glimpse. And lastly the dream of her voice, in which she was speaking:

> *My name is Kate*
> *I am an Irish girl*

My father died and not until he was dead did I learn that his mother had died in childbirth, in Ireland. Perhaps a narrative with all its light and weariness had forced itself upon me, perhaps it was all coincidence—though I am no longer willing to believe in *coincidence*—and in any case the names do not match, the dates do not match, and I am not sure in what country this happened, and this is perhaps only a tale told by the prisoner to the jailer. Perhaps the patterns of separate events containing certain details in common as to birth and death and origin, perhaps these overlie each other, and some light gets through into these dreams with which I lived then, in some terror, through the time my father was moving towards his own death. But that place of the dreams surely exists, where this narrative happened, where a man called Eli loved a girl called Kate who died of that love in a place called Watertown in the distant year of 1790. They were alive once; they were real fictions, the mask, the face, the voice. I no longer dream of him or of her, but years later, some years ago now, wide awake, I saw her clear as I see her now in the light, in a faded dress of grey cloth with small green flowers, her coat across her shoulders, her face thin and wiry, her shoes letting wet, coming towards me down the slope's loose stones.

Half songs, 1790

1

Saw you come down the shale, love,
the stones black in the rain.
In your hand a kerchief,
in that plain bread.

Your frock's all frayed,
your face white as thistle hair.
And the wildness in your face, love,
and the cold stood there.

Come down to the mill's lamps,
a May morning.
Peewit cried on the clover.
Saw you turn and turn.

2

Rain on the running hill's back,
rain on the mill's black side.
Nowt but trouble ails you,
you're no bugger else's bride.

The lovers meet in the marshland,
the lovers meet in the sky.
There's no one comes to meet you
on the black pit's other side.

But your face so pale and sleek, love,
and your eyes like a bird's, so sharp.
There was hunger enough till now, love,
but now there's never enough.

* * *

Wolf vision

At the abandoned farm
in the clearing shrunk
from the field it was,

woods of birch
and hickory sprung
from the forest's axing –

American trees still awake
in their Indian names,
old field measured out

in blunt immigrant speech –
I was a man with his dog
running out

on the snowclapped
glazed winter grasses
gone into scrubland.

Some look in his eye
not dog's but wolf's
pierced me. Running

again through the edges
of clearings the late
sunlight blazed in,

pond ice, bracken,
saplings risen again
from their winters, away

on some plain
answering only ourselves
we were wolves howling.

Hawk vision
(for Tom Nickerson, vanished Indian)

At Wachusett, the lake darker
through winter straight pines,
rocks dumped in the ice sheet,
we stood for a bird's high

hovering over the inlets: red hawk
like none the books mention
circled and lazed on the air's
updrift over his watching hold

down the cone of his vision
of stone and valley tight to his eye
that fed on a wide space of small
movement he's triggered by: snake,

rabbit: liquid shutting the lens
pinpricked down to his dive –
everything in him going in one
feather spread downflight first

on the fur-stripping claws
second his bone-splitting beak.
I should shudder, remembering
victims I've known, times

I've been killer, harbour gull
snapping off crabs' legs;
other times I was running
home through the evening, then

hunched by that knived
falling out of the light.
That day we were watching, part
of his landscape, a claw's length

out from the wars of ferrets
and eagles, land grabs, horse thefts,
slavings and sack of our separate
tribes, alert for his dive

but he circled. And rose
in a spiral upward into the blue
shock of the sky diving
somehow upward and vanished.

Remembering when he was a wolf

The light on the fields
slowly vanishing,
the old dark padding back,
the old sifting of dust.

I sat by the stone, rainspots
had pitted and dried. Here the wind
carries everything off:
seeds, names, old barns.

In such light we skirted the clearing,
sunset breaking across us. And ran
through the open, we howled
so the stones must hear us.

In the scrub leaf-mould thickened,
cold to my hands. I fell there,
the pack left me, heat of my body
left me, a briar whipping my cheek.

Creatures had dug in the frost,
their small breaths melting the ice,
little wandering pumps
chewing up leaves. I was a wolf,

my work to wait
till nightfall and catch them. It could be
my boots snapping sticks
through this wood is all I want now.

It could be that sitting here
with my black gloves on a stump
keeping my hands' shape
is what I always wanted.

Another night of muttering

and shaking, cat cries,
boots kicking in the alleys
and all night I swear someone
calling from far off *please
to come in.* I dreamed
nothing, I dreamed I was asleep
with the eyes of my enemy
watching.

The sun, skimming the mist off the marshes,
trees breaking through
like junked ships. At the tips of three sticks
of the wintered elm
three crows, like three
black flames.
That describes it. On the sea
a quick slap of sunlight, the day
set loose.
            In the street
early risers with flasks
and lunchbuckets set out
for the port. There is
nothing to tell you, the city
coming awake, everyone
pulls on the ropes, from a lifted window
a man shouts down his hands
such good little citizens.

Hard to say where I've been. One place
was a thin skirling music,
its own sound, rain
gusted through rocks,
Arab music the way they hear it.
They played, each his own song
with others, a joyful lament.
A girl danced, dark, skinny-legged.
Others stood to one side listening.
In a doorway a drunk
was taking a leak
and falling. When he sat up
he was spitting his teeth out,
a gob of whiteness.

Tales of Urias the shape-shifter

First he was stone, the great sleeper,
the company of other stones
was no blessing.

Stone-still he'd talk
with the white hurrying mane of water,
no one believes it.

Glimpsed in and out woods
following the beck, by the downrush
forgot all his words for water.

Then a bird was his lifting wing-shadow
dropped down the valley.

In his skull dreamed again smoke,
mill-waste, the cotton-spinners'
dreamless sleep, Pennines
dark and satanic, so he sang *Jerusalem*.

Man again, from gutturals
making his first sentence,
singing through looms and his grudging masters
all the songs of the settlement.

A country their god had forgotten
his blessing. The birds, they sing
once there and fly off
léaving no message.

By the stream of a Sunday
would he fish, court,walk and fight.
Some time in rage a frame-breaker,
speech-maker, read the London correspondence.

And with others come in the blue
withering light at day's edge
down the mill's shadow, some but six years
picking cotton waste, always hungry.

Brooding years after he'd ask
if a man believing in silence should talk much.
Went preaching, the book of black words
in his back breeches' pocket.

Till at evening his clogs
pounding the hillsides he's famous for
he's come to the praying hole.

Behind him the gap in the rockface
is the stone's mouth speaking through him.
The birds and the beck's noise
and his people around him are one sound.

Then with the voice that learned speaking
over the groan of flywheels
he's urged his half-fed congregation
up from the stones till over the magpie's screech
and the jay's the woods
fill with their shout *Hosannah*.

My father fading out

Each time I recall him he's grown
thinner and paler, *am I*
making myself clear he shouts
from the hearthstone, already

I see almost through him
asleep at the fire, exhausted
evening by evening, his crossed feet
pink and opaque at the open oven door.

If he slams out now it will be
fainter and shake the house less,
less curl to his lip for his bosses –
Reggie Rat, Charlie Woods, Wallace Dixon.

For them he went topping and tailing
bent through the frozen turnips,
or stooking in summer pitched his fork
high in the air in blind sudden anger.

Now he fades out, the wireless
plays him to sleep, he wakes, asks news,
sees in the coals the black flag of a stranger,
dozes again, then is gone completely.

Valley

Pale grass
a long flag
striped once by the river,
the one
wandering blue star
of the heron.

In the light's early silence
the farmers crank the old box Ford
full of chickens. The cock croaks,
he has counted his wives,
some are missing,
plucked and stiffening
under the market awning. Nothing else
but a pheasant's stuttering,
a distant bell sound. I see
in the starry river
the keel mark.

Tightened into the bank's
wooded side under the steep
hill's stone shadow
a Viking boat
is still vanishing.

Childhood in the lowlands

> *'Foweles in the frith,*
> *Fisses in the flod.*
> *And I mon wax wod:*
> *Mulch sorw I walk with*
> *For beste of bon and blod.'*

Hello
hello

into the mouthpiece
over and over

is anyone there?

But she would not speak
to him again ever
she tells anyone but him.

That's it she's gone.

He visits his childhood: tight,
wiry, a cable
hung in its own weight. One cheek
to the mountains,
fixed on Ben Ledi's snowtip.

One cheek to the underground weeping,
coal smell of a coal town,
image of a man
pinned beneath beams, his father
wriggling under the mountain.

Choppy water, white horses on the firth,
but no fishing in the flood.

Sunk Island, that winter

> *'O westron wind when wilt thou blow*
> *And the small rain down shall rain'*

O that my love O that
my love: the wind,
the reeds, the telephone wire
and I, all singing.

It's late afternoon
in a flat country,
the sea birds rise
far off and fall quietly.

But the sea goes away
leaving these fields,
this tall yellow marsh grass
and the small trees blown inland.

And last winter the gale
lifted the pigsty roof, the geese
blew out to sea, the bell
on the dull swell of the Humber

clanked through my dream
of hills in my own land.
Perhaps I am leaving,
a man stung by his woman's scolding.

Perhaps nothing. Or drunk
going home by the ditches,
singing, from a neighbour's house,
a man at the end of himself

where there's only the sea
on the sea, each thing at a distance:
dutch barn, brick letter-box,
wall of the house I will sleep in.

Old postcards of the river

View of the city with boats,
some rigged for a journey –
the canal, in watercolour, 1830.

Where the poor stew nettles and fennel,
all England affords them.

But these trees and sails
in the wide space, a woman
heaving a basket home on her shoulder
late in the daylight
seem to belong there.

If my country is slowly
lighting again,
its villages

opening their doors
and the neighbours waving –
that dream is soon over.

In the grey photograph
three who are
recently soldiers

grin from France
where they died
rifles aslant

at a slow pace, shoulder to shoulder
in perfect step, who
followed the piper

or huddled in mud
died in any case.
What for won't go

on a postcard. Fishing
down the canal
on Sundays

I find their initials
on stones
by the lockgates

standing easy together
just as they
left them.

In disbelief
at this new thing
the camera, workmen
freeze in the street,

one raising a stick
in suspicion, a boy
mocking and pointing.
Beside him a woman

dark in the face
as the sunless
underwing of a bird,
still turning away.

The swan

It happens, spring comes to the river,
grass freshens, the reeds remember the dry sound
last year's wind made amongst them.

These pollards, clubbed and splay-fingered,
are the same willows of my childhood.
These are the same birds
born over and over, rising in the estuary.

Then the swan flies, his wingbeat
through air a slow heavy applause
that ceases, sighting the weir to turn there,
takes his precise self in one motion
down to the furrow he's cut in still water.

The wholeness of him, feather by feather.
The white sail of a ship
gone long since to the horizon. Or the lance
of a returning crusader. Or
a white banner bearing perhaps good news
at last from the kingdom.

Playing field observations

In the light before rain
counting the hard little
yellows of the dayseyes I went
down the sea-opened valley –

a neat country it's said
of parkland and flood plain
squared like the blind man's garden
between the waters.

Sang goodbye to the elms,
glimpsed by the canal
blue smokey lift of a heron,
accepting my birthday.

How the shadows move in
at such news and are strange
in the light. This feather
left for his marker my brother

the crow had dropped by the goalpost
seems a dead man's finger
keeping his page
in the unfinished biography.

The Tivoli Bar

I look into the hole.
So this is where you live.

Mostly it's dark. When there's light
I look at things: the worm,
the dungbeetle hoarding his muck.

In the dark I remember him.
In the dark I have to imagine.
It's the only town left –
streets, people at tramstops,
and the eyes of young women
looking downwards.

In the dark
I roll out the words on my palms.

If I could spend them
I would spend them wisely.

I hope so. But I want
the quivering world that's in them
to pass hand to hand
between us.

Federico

They will come they will come.
They have been before.

I watched them, from my hole
under the thornbush.

The soldier's boots
were ringing in the yard.
No one's here
I told him.

Each time they come
I have to begin again.
If I don't remember, too bad.
And if they don't believe me
I'll say the truth anyway.

Wanting to shout wanting to say
go away go away.
Stop interfering with my silence.
Let me write my poem.

He takes it. Later
I see him squat by the wash house
and clean himself on it.
So take it.
Paper is scarce.
I'm glad he finds purpose there.

Take the poem. And if you
can use it
use it.

What I mean is: leave off,
I'm busy. What I want is
to close the gap
between writing the poem
and a letter to a friend.

Maria the thief

I stole the cup.

I stole the water.

So take them.

I confess everything.
On the other hand
I may deny it.

I stole the food, books, furniture,
clothing and shoes.
Though I paid cash
I stole it.
Though I worked for the money
I stole the work.

Give me what's mine,
air clean as the mountain,
the pine smell,
my allotment of rain.

Give me my portion.

Caesar Caesar

Soldiers must try hard.
They overrun one country
finding the frontier
a thousand miles further
still needs defending.

Such a profession –
soldiering.
And for the police
there's always work.

Where does it go?
All the bootleather,
sweat, curses, orders,
the lists
of those to be shut of,
those who take and are taken,
watchers and watched.

They come to the same place:
the round cry
dragging everything into itself.

Reports from the east

Days coming away from each other,
threshed out.

Stripped to the bone. Butchered.
The bones pounded to black dust
gold teeth are sieved off.
Trains, marshes, ashes. Some
request death, some walk into the wire,
one told to hang himself
took off his belt and did so.

Whether you will,
whether the clocks shedding
moment across moment record it
pain
comes to be fed, all the cries
to be uttered, misery's processions
to be numbered.

Or else
let there be singing, as at Janowska.
A fiddle, a whole orchestra
is given. We have to be thankful,
even one mercy, a raindrop for instance.

To survive

Each day the last,
each a survivor. A shaft
other days fall into.

Books, tables, lost objects
call back to us.
I remember my razor's edge,
the lift of my good bed.

Mine I said *mine*, doubting now
whether these fingers, these knees
would answer in my name.

A man assembled from nothings,
bones and tissues. He would eat,
he would swallow his name for nourishment.

At night the dark
looks out on itself, and the days pass,
a chain of black flowers.

Bowl

A bowl of soup.
A bowl of soup.

It is the hands
melded together, tip into tip.

Stains in the cracked enamel.
It is pure longing
where the soul bunches up.

Peelings and sawdust, a weak milk.
Compelled to share
she cups the heat into herself.

What the other takes
she measures in absences,
fills herself
in the warmth, in its lack.

Wants

Such effort to make ruins.

The city has emptied, footstep by footstep.

Grandfathers searching through clothes,
trousers and shoes, emptying cupboards.
The voices have left
and call in another place, anxiously.

They were neither fleeting nor wistful,
they struggled under the ban of the empire.
In my pocket on a torn piece of paper
is a word for *goodbye* in spidery writing.

I want the voices to find each other.
I want the parts of speech rising towards each other.

The veterans

Each with his president's telegram.
Each with his emblem, the grey bloody flag
he shows no one.

The medal the map the names
of his bullet-raked brothers, notes
of the book of delusions

he'll write now the war's done
and the empire diminished. *We
never gave it much thought*

is said of atrocity, cameras
noting his face, the mouth
that says it's a mouth in a face
that says it knows better now.

Now he's like everyone,
some days alone, sometimes anywhere,
with his woman who reads for him
books from the vanishing country.

Peasant

Flattening into the bank
as his lord rides by: not a man,
but a root of the elm
grown round stones.

In the field carrying straw
or straggling home beneath sticks
in failed light
two legs and a burden.

Lives in smoke, picks wheat
from the grainpit cracks,
limps through the frozen ploughland
turning an acre a day.

Dreams in flashes: rabbit
snared in the waste filched home
in his jacket, pheasant's
stuttering blur whose eggs he sucks clean.

And the boy he was with the oxgoad
tramped through the watermeads, first light
finding him still in that field
bent and ailing.

Water lifts off the land.
We are dancing.
We are not dancing.
He is a man, he is waving,

a speck in the falcon's round vision
that pins him dreaming
his master's cut throat,
the beating of ploughshares.

Duck at Haldon Ponds

At evening watches the duck
slow feeding the waterline.

Praises the duck. Such a fine
white miracle breasting the mayfly.

Green of her tail feathers,
space of her neck doubled in water
paddles off with my mind.

Ducks I have known.
Old duck mates of mine
inspecting the meeting of air and liquid.

Make no mistake, duck.
I'd like to eat you well cooked
one bell-battered Sunday in April.

And I'd wear your gorgeous feathers in my hat,
make a soup of the bones
and give your leftovers to the cat.

Fly

I woke hearing a fly
touched again to its sound
pelted into the window
trying to leave

for what was it

—something in sunlight that said
to wake now. Beyond that
pulsed and repulsed buzz
between two sheets of glass

a bird's one note

come back to the world brought me
out of long sleep. Love,
as you stir from your dream's
untrembling be still for me,

let me begin

my song for it sings moment
to moment love of you.

Lake

Freed now the lake turns
between shores distantly
heard from each other.
We walk by not on it, not

chancing the ice

drifting apart from itself
and lying like pond scum.
A month back the lake
I stood by spreading its bulk

cracked whipped and cried

and fought its bed: animals
stirring, seeds pressing out
from the milkweed's grip.
I heard the ice shifting

tight packed, it talked

I tell you. You don't
believe me perhaps.

Crocus

Leaf, green spear with white
driven through, old trackway
the fair women went, trailing
their coats. The flower

purple folded

and folding over such orange
as burns deep in coals.
New risen, beating home
ahead of forsythia's

sharp yellow fire.

Crocus glints among leaf mulch,
cornering spring, the yard's
premonition of poppy shoots,
mountain ash berry, little prints

of weeping birch,

leaf and eye. Crocus lifts.
I have news for you.

From the southern river

> 'The proper business of ageing men is to sit on gates.'
> – John Lyle

Writing in provinces
far from each other
or any star:
greetings.

If there's news
I'll tell you
everything changes,
for you also –

the way maybe a train
stops beside yours
as you were not meant
to stop either,

hoots
and moves on.

At first we can't tell
which is moving
but the mind
comes back to the body.

Where someone is always
staring between empty sheds
at the foxgloves
and the elder bush.

Winter occasions

Years clanking in buckets, more years
snuffling in ditches, danced at shearings
and pig killings, my life in the country,
my life in the village, the owl blinks
in the thatch, the fireback blackens.

I was a girl, the sun flamed in a sky
of thistles and hemlock shaken above me,
I lay down close to the water.
Winter in, winter out
the wind nags me. Now he's back
from long absence, his boots
at the scraper, a squire
off walking the parish muttering
hoofbeats on roads I've not travelled. In his sleep
knives clatter, armies gather,
storms rake the upland, a girl
goes singing a love song over the watermeads
or he's crying
    so then I've lost you,
    in the old river the moon
    is still glittering.

I had been
all these years a stone to him, a hush
in his city of streetcries, or a light
he'd snuffed once and would light again,
pleading he's sorry and such, head in a sling,
dragging his deaths like a whale
round with him. He's amazed
there's life in me, blood's thumped
breath and tongue to tell him

he's mocked with his art. And he'd thank
my long waiting to greet him,
my hand at the latch, glad and a fool
when he comes home stomping his feet
with a comment I've wrinkled and thickened,
but it's years since I missed him.
                                   I was
content and will be again glimpsing
through trees the river's loop,
poppy's glare, harebell weighed
on the wind's stir.
                   Celandine bleaches,
                   the cold field's bleating winter
                   but in age there's fire
he announces, surprised again
and again stares at his table
and taking his pen starts up
some tale of a woman
sixteen years a statue
because of a husband's jealousy,
and him wrong in the first place.

At the Western Beacon, the second of the songs of Urias

All this elaborate disguise.
No one's here
anywhere under Orion
and the new moon's cup of rain.

Light divided over the moor
in the fields of the bronze makers:
sheep, bracken, ponies,
stoney rainsodden furniture.

With a stone to break you.
With a stick's point
rammed through the ribs. Then came
farmers and hunters, scraping for tin,
setting stones it's a warning to cross still.

Back when the moon was the pale
banished wife of the sun
in the lost tale of the arrowmaker's vision.
All their tools, bones,
legends and gods are one wash
through the peat now.

Scoffed down a bird's share
of porridge and bilberry. Snarled
among scrawny cattle,
dogs and their stink
trailing after. Then gone to the city
whose names mean water, a people
calling themselves *people of this land.*

Among grey rocks
I took her, her eye
glimpsing a half county
stopped at the ocean: blue sheen,
two boats in the ancient distance
where she is the sea and she dances.

Moiré effect

What was always the vision
reaching for more of itself

had eluded me. How it
never included itself:

that we notice the high
turn of the bird in sunlight,

its grace
stuns me out of all thinking.

Stood amazed at the barley,
orchestra of the oat plant.

And came over me crossing the bridges
such immanence things have:

part of how the world thinks
so through us the blank
stuff of space knows itself.

* * *

TRISTAN CRAZY

'I have leaped and thrown reeds and balanced sharpened
twigs, I have lived on roots in a wood and I have held a
queen in my arms.'
  – 'La Folie Tristan' (Berne)

One for sorrow

On the ocean –
useless to say I was drunk,
couldn't help it,
useless to say any thing –
then I loved you.

Weeds on the sea, the horizon
adrift, waves' heave
hoisting the spray's flags, sea
loose & flinty, stone in its making.

I fancy I see animals,
bushes & rocks. In the motion
words I had seen
thrashed into nothing
that nothing gives back.

Only clouds, one
shaped like a raven. Sometimes
a skimmer, garbage picker,
bird's wing lifting away from the lifting.
I see everywhere the same
belled planet's edge.
And love you.

Two for nobody

How he was king
of these rocks
& gorse. Oh
he told me.

Granite country,
heather stiff
in the seawind
divided at Cornwall:

his kingdom. She
was a swallow
bringing one strand
of her swallow's hair.

His woman, part
of his stoney possessions,
ah but love
set her dancing.

And the rest: how
she sneaked off
to find me
out by the elder tree,

how again & again
in the two backed
beast dance we went
crazy & careless,

were found, hounded,
beaten & branded.
Ah well shrug the citizens –
lies, guilt & old grief,

betrayal & such,
an old song the wanderer
sings for his bread
& each time changes

he sings it. *Love love*
wherever love is
changing its sheets
come find me.

Three: tales of the hunter

I crouched, hands & knees
beneath thornapple, mosquito
seeding its eggs in my arm.

And waited. What I caught
I killed or brought
struggling home.

When I found my enemy
I cut him to pieces & went
singing & bloody by the rowans.

But you, love. Now shadows
cast trees & I'm contrary,
rain my fine weather.

By night I'm prowling
your moonlit flesh. You're all
legs, arms, owl cry

& leaping, love, the cry
in my throat some animal,
its life in its cry.

And I swim with the fish.
I fly with the raven. I go
with the shuddering creatures
into their darkness.

Four, being a prayer to the western wind

Without you:
the moon's failed waters,
lost wheats of the Sahara.

A woman hides in these syllables.
She goes singing and dancing
through fields of tall yellow to the sea.

But the pastures are an old grit in my teeth,
the eastern forests an ash and smoke.

I pick among shrubs
for one leaf of you. On the sea
or high in the treeless upland
where I almost hear you
the wind whines to itself
be thou with me love
the corn in its chaff, or where
have I heard it?

Ships, ports, wharves, men
leaning on the cathedral stones,
I've been everywhere talking to everyone,
no one has seen you. In the snowy north,
in Germany and on the Atlantic
amongst men who are gulls' feasts
and the dreams of carrion it's your face
I fail to find in mirrors and water.

Asleep I see you
walking as once you were by the river,
but awake sleep has kept you,
I'm miles away where I barely think
how your sounds are, and must come
round the world's other side
finding again the same strangeness
opens your face in the gates of the city,
the wanderer home in his bed again.

Five, which is here by the river

Windless days reeds
tall grasses
motionless

cormorant a shoe
opens his wings
heron a stopped blue air

kestrel a moment
standing in flight come out
love from wherever

boats turned over
like the hands
of sleepers come out

from the waterbirds
of the shadowy
waterclogged marshland

come see me here
by the river but you
where are you

among these reflections
these lights do you see me
throw a stick in the water

oh then come out love
and see me a face
in the water

Six: the wife's complaint

It's for love
they told me

& brought me
across the high sea.

In his rainy country
of haunted plumbing
& traffic
not a damn thing works.

If he's king
of these fields
& wants loving
what if I'm bored

as the moon
with itself,
tired & bombarded,
a waterless ocean.

Watching the ploughman
leading a white
ribbon of birds
to the world's rim

I'm sick of it all,
or I envy
the gull's
easy lift

& long to be
lost as the larks
in larksong
over the moorland.

These my hands,
first & last
those we love touch,
that in passage

from hairline
to heels
could make you forget
till in one

gathered up fire you lose
even your name,
sight of my face,
number you thought.

So then it's true
we're meaningless
here on the earth,
tupping & dying –

soiled sheets &
nailbitten bafflement,
his feet that smell
of old wood,

cradling his head
crying love love me
till death
for through us

nowhere is somewhere,
someone is running
here in the space
otherwise empty.

For a husband maybe
I'm rope, coiled
& used, no doubt
I'll be used again.

For another I can
be woman to man:
Tristan, Isolde,
Isolde, Tristan.

Seven: when he can't sleep for thinking

Other nights of muttering,
knives scraping stones,
wanting through grunts
& half sleep to kill anyone.

Won't where he can't bear
for its loss his possessing her,
beside her thinking who else
had called through her hair

his little death's loneliness,
beached on that shore
his mind ends, and she
spent & howling.

Gossip, a thornbush. My bird,
stay with me. Her voice
a blaze in his skull.

In his mind digs a pit
& burns her, surrounds her
with razors, broods over
footprints & stains.

Love makes some sing
& shrinks some. Brings down
his fist & will own
what he can't own in women.

Or else raffle her, give her away
at the street corner,
the prize in the lepers' race

but have done anyway, take off
& damn her to hell, slam the door
forever shut after him. She sleeps,
in her pink flesh, beside him.

Eight. The singer

Nights when he is
peering through mist
at the ship breaking
coast & would be there.

A flat song: the warrior
scowling under the helmet,
a girl, her breasts
of white china clay,

nights on the wire
where his body rotted,
an example to all
in those trenches.

In spite of the knife
the club the fire
to burn him, the gun,
he would go back crazy

where she's anyway
forgotten him. He sings
show me the wind's seam
or a lovelier woman.

Continents, rivers.
A vain young man
is the singer, the
peacock, singing

oh love oh love
a mire so muddy
who'd walk there?

Nine: Shorty's advice to the players

In the flinty upland
of sheep & ravens
they dreamed
each the other's vision: birds,
these flowers bursting
a thousand years back
tramped in the battle's muck.

Forget the knights –
a fist on a field of azure,
his lady, her feet
on the chained swans, not able
to turn the stone cheek to his cheek & cry,
he would not, small
in his armour,
tender as mollusc,
stone in the cathedral.

Hitched her skirt
on his lancepoint, laid her down –
not first, last,
nor long remembered. Went,
bum, singer, a fool, the black
furious horseman, nothing worked out.

His death: full of briars,
a black sail a white sail he's glimpsed
in the magpie's jittery flying.

Little brother
she won't ever come back now.
Get used to it.

Ten: the tale unfinished

At the end there's no love
without death comes along
with the wedding dress,

in the ring on the bridegroom's
midnight finger; either way
there's death, bleak as that bird

that's king on his stonepile.
So I shrugged and loved you.
Your face sings now in my head

where without you I'm snail
dragging his tongue across stone,
I'm the bell that rings

in its own windy space, I'm out
with the ageing light
of the stars and as lonely.

And we're not love, each
as we each imagine, more lost
in each other's distance

wearing our separate flesh.
Other times with the gift
of your moving sometime with me

I am out of all mind, and recall
your running all gooseflesh
towards me. As you ran

I thought how you were
a message folded like prayer,
delivering itself.

* * *

FUN CITY WINTER

For Annie for whom
these were
love poems perhaps

A red carnation

Winter in Fun City. The Laughing Sailor, the dodgems and
the bingo boards sheeted down, spray flung over the harbour
wall. I investigate the dike, the cliffs, Oldtown and the
priory church, a great East Riding farmer's barn, or a merchant's
notion of what church ought to be, its vault stacked with
spent prayers. After some centuries the tithes and rents and
rights of pannage and verdure amount to these same stones,
I think, and shut the door on it. Each day I visit my mother
in the hospital, I stay in her house and order its affairs under
the eyes of her lodgers, the young policeman and the French
assistante, who seem almost aware of their symbolic presences
hovering in the background. Everyone here is old, retired,
living by the sea, even the young, you remark, visiting. One
day I make a detour to visit my father's grave, and lose
myself among the brick semis. I cannot ask. Everyone I pass
is old. I cannot ask them the way to the cemetery. I find my
way at last, and on the grave I place a single red carnation.
So this is he that raged and broke crockery all through my
childhood, and on the morning of my wedding, years ago,
stamped on the flower—a carnation—spitting *that to your*
buttonhole. So this is he.

The town, a general description

Boats, harbour swell, bone-cutting wind
off the bay, and far inland
noise of the sea beating on stones.

I sit under the nightstar writing my music.
Winter's a cry in me
that I loved you, here in a country

childhood blurs down the telephone wire,
dark with the deaths of friends, their news
coiled on the flat gull-hunted landscape.

* *

The headland in dawn light
whitens. Boats fishing the bay mouth
glitter, bird followed.

By Danes' Dike the larks
threw down song. A harebell glimpsed
in the land wind was the pale stare

my grandfather grew, years at sea
seeking this landfall, its waves
folding the first of the light

where in death his eye
pearled as the eye of the caught fish
glazes on land, the sheen off him.

* *

Centuries back they walked off the sea,
sour and Danish, wanting
the green sea-glimpsed littoral,
battle-keen and bloody at the ebb mark of the bay.

Still dour, in a tone they have
of a slighted people, short
under the easterly. And whose history
if anyone knew was to complain –

the townsmen's daughters gang-raped
under the fish quay, and him
with his head stoved in
still haunting the foggy landing.

* *

I can believe a time my father
sulked up and down furrows
cursing his masters. Black his face was
on the white upland of the Wolds.

By Flamborough the leathery sea
gutters again in my vision. Each day
I visit and stare, calling it
grey tongue, bell clapper.

I write. I drink whisky.
I loved a woman. I write
this shell shaped like an eye is a shell,
this stone shaped like a heart is a stone.

* *

Sea grey with fog, white
with my father's spent anger, frost
nagging its offices, lugging his grudge

home through the evening. The place
I come to bury my dead is at street's end
the old sea falling endlessly

into my childhood. And is all
that's flawed and stoney in me
by these graves and this long water.

Where that time is a bird gone
from its birdbones. Where I won't stay.
Where the sea wears out its stones.

* *

I return. The sunlight through amber
is the bar at the Alpha Café.
The radio plays old dance records.
I visit the pinball machines in Fun City.

On the late night box it's Renoir
singing: *bullets fixed bayonets*
the single shot of a pistol
to bring down one man with a tin flute.

Ten o'clock watching the cars go by.
If we flew in each other's dreaming
in my skull I was with you
to whom these were love poems I guess.

* *

You moved I saw covies of birds
glide through the reeds. You sang
I heard waves break. Your name
called itself at a distance.

You with the sea strength.
You from the land of green ginger.
You in the wind in your dress
a flag with its shook sound.

Now moving with ebb sounds
moving with tide change
in the 5 a.m. river on sleep's
sisterly arm you wake and break over me.

The stone gatherer

Most days you see along the leftward curve of the bay slow figures in black treading the waterline, keeping their distances from each other. They are the stone gatherers, filling their pockets with smooth chalk pebbles, some mottled by seaweed, some blue or brown veined with ancient seepage, some holed through where in the chalk's softer places sucking creatures had dug down on the one leg of their lives beneath shells, and after them sandgrains had lodged and milled through, thrashed in the seawash. The stone gatherers take a few pebbles each day, and store them for neither purpose nor profit in their houses. Often enough their habit is a source of domestic irritation as the gatherer's obsession continues; it is a lifelong and silent activity. When a stone gatherer dies his collection is dumped, stealthily, and returned to the beach. A stone gatherer must collect his own, and only as a significant gift is a stone ever passed from one collector to another. They are solitaries. They rarely meet. They have little to say. Walking into the middle distance we see one of them, ponderous and dark, coming up the beach. Occasionally he turns to the water, staring over it as if he expected some solace from it. Occasionally he stoops to examine a stone or a shell or a bit of wave-smoothed glass. Occasionally he selects a stone. Nearer, in close-up, we see him holding such a stone upright on his flattened palm against the distant headland. Old holes cut through have broken it from a larger stone, and sea-turned it is a little figurine: a head, a body, limbs folded along itself, a hole through its middle: an embryo or a relic. Closer in we see between thumb and forefinger a little earth mother, and through its middle hollow the distance of bay and cliff and rising gulls, fading out.

By the northern sea, a farewell to one woman

Your face, frame in a frame of itself
in the train window, moved off
and the northern sea fog swallowed you.

I played a pretend violin
in the train station quartet. In a Bogart movie
I walked the length of the platform.
In my mind we went
by separate roads up love's stoney mountain.

Then at the sea's grey side
I was running under the moments.

In each you were miles off
on the flat grain of the ploughland, half weary England
beaded with rain, white gulls
on the fenceposts.

In each then I wanted you
as the yawning fish on the boatmen's slab
might say of the ocean. The want
swam away into nothing,
the sea in its envelope.

I'd have lived in the hollow of your shoulder.
I'd have been an idea in your skull.
I'd have read only the book of your name
never knowing what nights you looked out from.

My life turned on its mast in that town
years ago as that moment turned towards this.
Now I no longer want.
I recall only the North Sea chill
my voice becomes mist in.

* * *

APOCRYPHA FROM THE WESTERN KINGDOM

1. Six items heard in three locations in Leeds and
   Exeter

All I really wanted
if you really want to know
was a bigger violin.

*

So there was I
I'd painted 24 pictures
but they hadn't given me a wall.

*

And anyway it's daft my being an Irishman
not knowing how to fish.

*

I'm late because
the motorway was leaking,
so far you've shown
one grassblade of sympathy,
so I'll tell you what I will do
I won't shave.

*

I was in the hospital,
I said don't bring anything,
he brought me gin, daffodils, bananas.
I thought I'd never get out. .
One day I'd die there in the rainy city
having written my epitaph
three score and ten
my heart ten cents a dance

among the small intrigues,
amongst the provincial incests.

*

On the sign in the window
at the bus station office
in some northerly town

seen in the news that night
on the TV in our front room
it said

the next mystery tour
will be to Rosedale.

2. At the collège des beaux arts Escanceaster six further items imagined

25 years dedication to the virgin
man and boy and never once
had anyone acknowledged it.

*

Can't you see I'm weary
working all day
for the last half hour
on my thesis the great work
the book of lost arrivals
the library of last resorts
a definitive history of alienations.

*

Not worried not moaning
not whingeing
not whimpering in the corner

demanding one last cigarette
one last whisky in the New Victoria
once again the fandango
under the glitter of the turning dancehall ball
till the musicians dismantle their instruments
driving off in a white VW

crying *nobody here is making me an egg sandwich*
so who am I?
where am I going?
what am I doing here?

*

Schism, rebellion, grumblings
over coffee, strange alliances,
manifestoes, knives in the dark,
religious upheavals, slander,
fanatics under arms, chance,
palace coups, gossip, non-
aggression treaties, cults,
independence movements, the wind
weaving through the wheat,
client kingdoms, petty republics,
nods to the blind man, winks,
signs under the table, flags,
beasts, bureaucrats, piles,
foreign syndicalist ideas, –
all these bother the emperor.

*

Skin of my hands the colour of cut wood.

Summer over before it began.

Whistle at the heart's finish,
bottom line at the end
of the cardiograph's calligraphy.

*

Otherwise the wind is itself,
the birds are.

        In the wide space
a woman heaving a basket
home on her shoulder.

3. Surprised again beside the river

Among obscurities, gleanings
of my life's junk and scribble: 'Boats
there'll be son, and small wading birds',

bright swans, line of poplars
fingering out the western sunlight,
windows guttering the last gold.

This is all one tale that tallies.
This is one history, all my life
same old lament for a lost country –

the same music repeating gulls,
reeds, willows, small waves
slapping in the seawind, a landscape

such as Isca the river's, the town
brisk with traffic, the treeland thriving,
streets rained on and Sunday

in the western city I called home
I abandoned. Where my heart knocked
thinking *wave, wave, high salt crests*

I'm to cross again. I'm a face
not seen any more, not waiting
between trains any more, my absence

no longer recalled on streets
falling steeply to the river crossing,
ancient trackway to the tide's head.

Merchants and shipmen, dyers' huts
now timber shards in the damp flood level
the Saxons kept the Celts to,

Frog Lane tanners, dealers in hide stink,
boats that breasted the salt plains
of the sea's pasture far from any land

gathered in the basin, sails furled,
so many birds resting on the long passage
from anywhere to anywhere.

Isca the water: *uisque. Pisces*
the fish: place of fish settled
by the Keltoi, the beaten Dumnonii

before Vespasian built the road
at the garrison's muddy footing,
Mithras scowling in the rock face,

chorus of Dalmatian oaths,
dog latin. More cries after,
Germanic, bleak guttural Danish

hacking out throats, breaking
the townwall and burning. The town
clung on its hill, a queen's gift

so they'll tell you, *semper fidelis*
when the Conqueror had a man's eyes,
at the West Gate peasant rebels

struggling in the open sewers,
travellers on the causeway
of the never ending landscape.

Then Dutch William. Plague,
cholera, bread riots, ecclesiasts'
vendettas, knives, women, money.

Life to life I think I return there,
cuckoo's call in spring
drags my heart out.

Nothing lasts, nothing changes,
nothing's learned from the centuries
beyond the same brotherly betrayals,

the same wifely infidelities,
same defeats, same failures, same
journey into exile, at the mind's edge

landscape carried on the long roads
remembering red clay hills
reared green and wheat again,

the townsmen's prospect, white barn
distant cresting the land's line
under the long wind off the Atlantic.

Days are soon done. Sickness or age
or the sharp edge of vengeance
have us at the end. The tale holds.

4. Some unfinished movements

Whangleather he said. Stopped halfway out of the Volvo, one foot touching the pavement, her white face swimming his way in the half dark: *And what's that?* she demanded to know next.

Whangleather he repeated, turning the ignition and stepping into the evening to tell her over the car's roof: *That's something that don't come apart in the rain the way you do.*

*

'The record office,
here or somewhere about' –
a tall brisk man in a beard

swinging the blackthorn
gives the library trees
a swift dressing down.

*

I didna sleep all night
I was throbbing
I was bad bad bad.

Long ago, a long way back,
far away from any place,
the very centre of the universe
blowing a dandelion clock
beside the river for instance.

*

Takes his supper at the bar.
Takes his wallet out to pay for it.

Opens it she thinks
like the Book of Common Prayer.

Sets his knife fork plate
down in front of him, salt and pepper,
mutters *and I hope it chokes you.*

*

The Wages of Sin is Death
saith the black spraypaint of the underpass.

The Wages of Sin are Death
it says underlined twice, underneath.

*

As for that red rainy ploughland
beyond the town wall
twenty centuries distant

that must be the other world
of the hawk's eye alert
and the grass in its moment.

5. Old business: the drowned bride

So you're back, your face
rising whitely up through the reeds
and the black bulk of you after.

Eloquent in your silence as ever.
The bell of your waterlogged body
tolls on the slow turning river.

And you won't come up from the weeds.
And this time I won't come back for you.
You would pull me in after

where you went down the rivermouth
through the cat-tails gobbling codeine.
Now you either go out in a new life

or drift on in my watery sleep.
So you nudge me awake each day
you're the light's first bitter thought.

You refer to your death
as *old business*, your laugh
laughs on in my head.

You say how the garden flourishes,
the town's found new meat for gossip,
and the children ask after me.

You say. The telephone rings,
the day begins, your voice arrives
and divides the air and I hear you.

6. A right curse on the enemy

Still around I see, still drunk,
still barely upright singing *Lily of Laguna*,
still hanging by your shirt tail.
Even though you're dead.

I don't know how you do it Jimmie.
I really don't. Shiftless. Lord Wistful.
We called you Alexander Impecunious,
forever borrowing two quid till Friday.

I've listened to your heart
that never spoke, felt no pulse
thumping in the dead wrist
where I placed lightly my finger.

I've pronounced you deceased
late kicked the bucket shuffled off
gone forgotten joined the elder brethren
with the great architect at last.

I've held a clear mirror to your face,
sent round a wreath, cancelled your subscription
to the Society of All Mates Together,
put your name in the obituaries.

And I've assigned you to the past of verbs.
You with your skin the pallor of dead water.
You will not paint. You will not fish.
You will no longer love the salmon leaping.

I've imagined you amongst the dead,
handing in your keys to the desk clerk,
handing in your name and loose change
still protesting you were innocent on Earth.

No one is. We lie to those we love,
we do not love them. Or else
we learn we cannot lie in love,
we cannot love ourselves or anyone.

So you're a man who cannot love himself.
You're a man selling salt to the sea.
You're a dead language and you its only speaker.
You're a joke in the museum of broken marriages.

And you broke mine. This is my revenge.
What else have I to do? I want
to stand beside your grave and find
some little good to say of you.

I'd like to feel compassion soon.
I want the luxury of some suspicion
I was wrong never to trust anyone since.
I can't until you're dead. So die,

old ghost, old misery,
you would have killed me anyway you could.
You betrayed me out of fear.
You tried very hard to destroy me.

So you were down, so you were beaten,
you were weeping in the bar-room,
you were skulking in the western wind
still crying for your childhood in the lowlands.

Old fox.
Got your tail in the water.
Now you die at last.
Here with this form of words. With these:

I feed you to the rain.
I sail your ashes down the wind.
I fade your name among the grass.
I think of you among the vanished.

* * *

The clearing

*

    Off in woods
a field that was tilled
isn't now: tall grass
decades deep, a caesura
birdsplit in the space
wind makes at the middle of continents.

Minnesota perhaps. Far enough,
his axe blazed the four corners,
making his own space his.

Ploughed it. At its edge
sighted his furrow on white birch
in the elm dark, the wheat
climbed his sleep
tensed as rigging.

By the stream. His face
swims there, child again
in the old speech.

As if any thing were finished,
summer gone, snow falling forever.
The magnolia stands
in pink fallen petals, a girl
shedding clothing.

Crossed the field,
sat by the water sighting
a boat come to shore –
crossed masts caught in the hawk's span
slid through his memory.

Blue jay, kestrel a rag in air,
the pheasant's yell wakens him,
rusty wheel through the bracken.

For him the wheel turned.
For him the corn the wind bowed
groaned in the millwheel,
then the bright stones lichened over.

In his ship on the pool
sails of a child's puzzle
assembling into a landscape.

He is standing again
at the seaport weeping,
the ship crowding sail
prowling over him.

*

      Where he ran,
bare heels through cowclap.
In the pond scrubbed himself naked.

Shy, nervous,
she'd not take her knickers off,
lay for him in the deep leaves.
It's not innocence
the fathers suffer from,
crouched in the birches, watching.

Then all his life scowling,
darker, cursing the crushed thumb,
land always resisting, forest
pushing in, pushed back
his share of winters. Years
distance lengthens down he recalls
her white thighs, peach fur
of her arms round him, pink moment
of her breasts spring wakens
year by year in the magnolia.

No use now he worked, broke
stone's weight dragging
harrow and plough. That he got sons
to farm after, fight,

curse him in snarls
they'd gotten from Vikings,
that their women toughened
and won't take his handswipe,
all means nothing. That the last
of his kin died beyond lonely
among byres and chickenshit,
the life grudged out of him
means no more. Though I can't hear
their immigrant speech, can't see
their scowl from the house
wanting me gone, there's some thickening
of air I walk through.

No use to die broken. No use
holding on to what suffering
holds us.

I am a cry among cries
in the field where I dance.

*

Hawk born from the wolf's mouth

Among sumacs, grey men
pushing their young before them
into the clearing, goldenrod, milkweed,
the space always mine now.

There is the young grass
shined by the wind, sun's broad light
as it was in the field
once when I was wolf.

Seeds passed, tumbling
their ways to wherever, the air
bringing smell of my brothers,
striking the howl in me.

I ran, the leaf shadows on me.
Bird crossed me, its shadow
swallowing the gnat's shadow,
above me the hawk's flight

formed in the updraught. I ran
through thin woods across water
the light trembled over,
wolf again, running.

*

Concerning the clearing

I carved faces in stumps. I set them to watch the clearing
below the stream and pond. I set them at the corners where
the man that farmed that field had stood watching his crops
under the weather. That man was long dead, leaving his
litter of chickenwire and bolts, a tip of tax demands and
foreclosures and smashed furniture, the house as he had
lived in it and died, gone to mildew, yellowed out. In the
field he had cleared was one great stone he had never
moved, a granite thumb. All his grown life he cursed it. He
would stand on it, a man cut off by the tide, safe on his rock.

An immigrant, a Swede. A man breaking his fingers on
stones he dragged off. In the dark house of stones: his
woman, his sons, his daughter. A living somehow, farming
the woods, turning the stream for dam and pond, lugging
stones into walls. The thumbnail blackened and fell off.
Cows mooned through the trees, huge and nun-like, breaking
sticks, lowing before rain. Pigs, chickens, a turkey for
Thanksgiving, a goose for Christmas. They were there perhaps
two generations, their last efforts abandoned chickencoops,
the barn fallen thick with briars, the space of a small kitchen
garden, abandoned. Old iron implements shedding into rust,
the soil faintly red, grainy flakes.

Up Bjorgen's Road above the city by the nuns' house. The
place is secret, mine despite the little red ribbons marking
off the plots that will be houses, developments on the edge
of town. A place of private rituals and the continuing presences

of those who called it their own, a space amongst others I
can open in my mind to walk there, to return, all my days,
where my mind briefly cleared of all its luggage and the
hawk turned sunward.

A field of grass. A long slope the sumacs advance across.
Through the elms the white glint of birches.

*

      Water's quick tongue
keeping its skin
of shaking branch, sky, reflection
waterbugs stride on, leaf floats.

I am where I am some animal
hunkering down in itself
to drink at the stream and stare
the unbreakable silence down.

Where the birds settle –
woodpecker's throb, dove's moan,
the cardinal's blood jet
as it would be without me.

To be still, a grassblade
dividing the wind, a monk hears it
steering his ship of the quiet,
his ear cupped to the stars,

in the ringing anvil of space
a bird with the birds. Three there were
at tree height driving the hawk off
his wings thrashing out sound

not part of him, not built
to fly among crow nests but hungry,
weary, wrong-muscled,
grey bird of my death

folding himself in the tree
a long moment above me hiding
demanding my silence, the watcher
watched. He stares now

in my mind catching his breath
into me, as if he were my death.
Flies again, driven out, crows
and the sunlight after him.

*

      Elm, birch, evergreen
above snow's remnants, the young firs
lost in spring, leaves
clenched through frost, folding out.

Among birches, families of five
sprung together, some lost
and some winter broken, survivors
gathered in old parchments, their skins'

weathered alphabets, pitted bark
of lost writing, lost marks,
a language left in the baggage trains,
stolen from docksides.

Tell me it's so. We remember.
Tell me someone remembering us
sitting out in the last woods
warms our old cheeks.

In water, in the greenness
under reflections I'm stolen away
waking years later among elm roots
again nodding to the ferns.

And speak again. Or nothing.
Or, children, holding the cup
drink from it, in a kingdom
to which I was travelling.

* * *

FOX RUNNING

*'who could release a woman
or dream there was a key'*
        – Tom Pickard, 'Window'

Fox
running
loose in his sleek skin
loose in his slick fur

Fox
between lamp dark and daylight
loping through the suburbs
miles bridges canals rails

Through the town littorals
chicken runs long bricked over
wild places put to the plough

Streets keeping their tilt
and curve of old lanes
over Crouch Hill into Seven Sisters

Through Haringay Hornsey
Highgate Holloway the cold
wind of the subway tunnels

Out under the sky Highbury
Hampstead to Paddington
among the grey yellow bricks

Chimneys and flat house fronts
his London skyline, pencil
of the Post Office Tower
his marker for Baker Street

Along the bottom line
of Regent's Park for Camden
hiding out along the waterway

Fox
ranging the city's inner spaces
being scavenger of skips parks
and desirable period residences

Fox wanting to be alongwind
amongst bracken his own shade
the breeze at his back

One eye sleeping, shut
on some chicken dream of wire
and bloody feathers in his nostrils

One eye awake to his hunters
and the slavering jaws
of the hunting dogs, his brothers once

Being outlaw
out classed out priced out manoeuvred
hunger leashing him in to the city
in the rattling milk bottle dawn

Back of his mind brome blowing
wind sifting the oak leaves
back of a stone littered silence

Back of his fox skull
mountain ash and the wide sky
printing his memory's tape

In at last from the wide
improbable country the townsmen
gape at uncertain such space
ever was for running: the fox

Aloof distant alert
holed up between running
in his red slash of fox body
running from the emptied distance

Crowded with townspill
of building sites' muddy footings
where will be flyover
industrial estate new bungalows

Years ago long ago late he is
skin of his name of his legend
skin of his alias son of his alibi
son of his tale told for children

Running into the tube maps
into the bus routes into the rails
learning the districts
learning connections and running

Into the city
dawn glimpsed and sometime sighted
I've seen him running
from Lancaster Gate to the Long Water

Poor winded breath shortening
and his thatch thins, wanderer

Running into his death
and his death always with him

Running into the razor
heart attack up his sleeve
shotgun pepper in his backside

Fox writes:

From a small room writing small
between the lines in the margins
on the one book left to me, *Vallejo*

in spidery lines of joined up writing
in case I shall need them
all the words for *goodbye*

Between the image and the next
instant of the image the trace
on the retina: a man bouncing a ball.

He is naked, jerky, long ago
his handsome body fed the ground.
Sunlight on him then

is the travelled light our star
sows in the thin electron milk
where will be galaxies.

Your attention please. I shall offer
a small gob of advice: *listen.*
Listen to the sounds listen
to the music listen to the fox.

And look at the pictures: our man
in the Victorian back yard
opening his fist to throw the ball

is a ripple of overlapped slides,
still frames of himself running silently
up and down in his birthday suit.

Where we see him we never would have.
In black and white.
In the space we occupy. Here.

Called *persistence of vision*,
the image on the retina a space.
Called retinal memory: the ball

through the white blur of rebound
falls to his hand closing round it
all the years since:

a fuss of white dove feathers.

Beginning again and again
beginning from what's broken.
Nights trying to slip under sleep's door
under the backwash of images:

her voice, how he turned
years through the black mill of her hair.
Came to this: nights on the stairs
not knocking on any door.

Half a morning round the phone box
before picking up the black handle.
Glad the line's busy, no one home.
Glad the number's off the hook.

All the lines through Bristol out.
From the number in his name no answer.
Outside the winter city, Maida Vale
glimpsed grainy pictures of the rain.

Wears his gasp and hunch of defeat,
his button saying *out to lunch*.
At Paddington debating trains.
In Kilburn disorderly and drunk.

Hunting alone between the city north
and the city south of the river.
In Brady's Tavern with a cash flow problem
exchanging alcohol for coin of the realm.

Twice around the Circle Line.
At Waterloo the last train north
to Camden, scattered roads of bottles,
VP and cider empties, upturned crates.

Holed up with Baudelaire and Lorca.
On Sundays picking up exotic fruit
along the market side, selling
half a dozen ties he's nicked.

Back of Dingwalls where the lads
were selling junk. His mad and
staring eyes. His mouth
repeating how she was his sparrow.

How she was his woman, faithless
as the wind turns anywhere, he'd been
better bedded with the wind
or wedded to the water.

Winter and summer all he loved
lied to him when he'd not
hurt anyone would he. Such
were the gaps in his schedule.

Such were his night thoughts.
Other nights he'd off himself,
fall into the rail, take his last
white skittering glimpse of England

down Beachy Head cliffs. Stain
the rocks. Feed the ravens.
Such was his nightly scenario,
his single movie of himself.

Happens. Crash. The fall from grace
blind drunk into the orchestra,
the bit where she sits peeling daisies
saying she loves him loves him not.

Sleepless. Nights the twenty years
of loving her are all one string
of beads on mother misery's rosary,
and how she knew to put the boot in.

And put the boot in. Lists his one last
broken wedding dish, his one last cry
in any corner, his one last cigarette,
under the glittering dancehall ball

their one last tango, one last fuck
anywhere under the stars and how
when his mouth said yes to her
there was his penis saying *no no no.*

His single ticket to the city,
a room, nights howling in the shower,
sleeping drunk inside the wardrobe,
dreamless, pissing in the sink.

And wakes to the same black anger.
Wakes to the same blank hunger.
Wakes to the same bleak search
for some fox warmth to his fox flesh.

Years, tickets, trains. Mewling
the same bleached nothings
on the salt roads anywhere, fears
he'll live lonely, die alone

in some white room in white linen
where death's angel pulls the plug
and if there's any last word of him
only she hears it: efficient, crisp,

antiseptic, laying out his body,
informing his relations, turning up
the watch at her lapel noting
time of his departure.

No way.

No way a fox goes out, no way
a man who was fox, kept ignorant
of what killed him, icy in the morgue,
ashes in the crematorium, words

entered in the black form filed away
beside the red his birth was
and between some forty years
his blood pumped out of him

the skylines that he crossed,
his memory of ferns and rivers,
distance, open country, city,
women that he loved, songs he sang.

Better die quick, if fox
at the heels of the hounds, if man
at the razor of some loonie. Better live
and if living running better run.

And keep running. Marylebone,
Lisson Grove, Edgware Road to Kew
to Wimbledon. Scattered sparks
and windblown newsprint, coming out

surprised again beside the river,
images the city has, home
the subway's groan and slide of pipes
and checking out of maps, his skull

encountering the city, his body
moving with a certain grace,
moving with particular intelligence
across the city's interstices.

And surviving through the rooms
his flesh joins other flesh
and makes some heat. Among
the endless conversations, starts, stops,

unfinished lives' biographies,
feints, gestures, cries, his life's
plain furniture, a borrowed room
in Camden to begin again from nothing.

Thoughts of a man around 40.
Notes. Maps. Things missing.
People that he loved his life ran with
all gone now, gone forever.

Just as they should be.

As they were meant to vanish
between here and the last hillside.

Between this space
and the next loneliness.

Between the image and the next
clear instance of the image
the retina remembers:
a man bouncing a ball.

Remembers how he was then
Fox
running in his long blood anywhere

early morning out
down the stairwell

sighting in the betting shop mirror
running just like him
with his same fox cunning
his brother

turning up his coat in rain
dodging in the underground

down the iron stairs at Camden
at King's Cross up and down the escalator
up the iron stairs at Goodge Street

following the lights
following the signs

running slow
running quick
in the stale winds trains shift
through the underground veins
of the city

Earl's Court to Barbican
by seven different routes

blinking briefly in the light
sniffing briefly in the air

investing in the breweries
his last Isaac Newton portraits
and never coming up all day

cashing in his cash card
ripping up his cheque stubs

waiting for his giro
arguing his earnings related

always with the wrong form
in the wrong office
on the wrong floor
of the wrong building
in the wrong part of town

and anywhere and anyway
wrong
plain wrong

we're afraid
Mister Fox
you don't qualify
for any sort of benefit

screaming back
so you sign it
you sign it Puffadder

running
running

up and down the moving staircase
in and out the tunnels

longing for the girls
saying underneath they're all lovable
being hetero and macho and lonely

his head full of underwear
his head full of skin

when he sees

in the opposite direction
running just like him
with his own fox longing
and his own fox cunning

himself

his face all surprise
his own foxy stare
carried off in the onrush
in the opposite direction

running with a wave
with a flickered recognition
beginning of a gesture
running

flying off on the train in the black
and its wind all around him
sniffing on the platform

and no one to tell
that he's seen him
Fox
his double
in the mirrors
his brother
himself
who'd anyway believe him

who'd anyway tell him
nay you're just pissed Jim

Between the image and the image
and the next motion of the image
Between the seer and the seen

Between the moment and the moment
Between the next and the next
Between denial and the fact

Between the running and the running

Comes the memory the space
Comes the man with the ball
Comes the one still space
for a brief time
in the city

Fox writes:

Tommy's space, crow nest
up the stone spiral into the wind
to the room at the house top.

Among plants and words I mellow out
watering the avocados Jascha your lady
has brought from their stones.

Avocado, *aguacate, ahuacatl*, testicle.
Above the rainy city peopled
by late quick footsteps
along the park's night edge.

Midnight. Clocks shedding
at variable distance the several sounds
of another night halving the planet
is one fancy English way to say it:

the silence, discovering itself
in what measures it at last
beyond failure, the black long ditch
welling with its dead with their mouths

still muttering their loves.
I'm alone, I have slept, I wake
from my own long wanting to die
eighteen months I can say that.

142

In my dream I put down the phone,
I said *that was a long time ago*.
I woke to the night's hard frost
and the dark city sleeping around me.

The planet sailed on through the nowhere.
It was the beginning of the last two decades
of the century called twenty, as reckoned
by the Europeans, I being one

of the northern hemisphere, this sector
the lights and the radio sounds
seep into space from, chatter
of our making some sense here.

By the park, where the nightjar is singing.
The voice breaking cover is mine,
the background hiss creation's
continued explosion. All the rest

being static on the tape and the airways,
late incoming plane from elsewhere,
traffic slowing to the Parkway.

Between the image and the next
sure moment
between the image and the next

Where I ease the dial station
to station, anthem by anthem.

Moscow. AFN. Stray voices
through the all night small hours

on the short wave, cop lullaby,
ship to ship interception,

quick blast of Securicor Cockney,
static crackle, long music

and two words repeated:
her hair, her hair, her hair,

some patches of silence, some
rapid reply to an unheard question,

tooth decay projects in Africa
on Voice of America, bulletin,

bluegrass, Chrysler, Jesus
through the late 3.00 a.m. shift

till first light shivers awake
one then two birds then the orchestra

of wide awake bells and the wolves
in the park begin howling for meat.

All night in the radio dark
the opinions arrive, urgent

hooded versions of history. From Kiev
Hangchow long grain statistics,

Sofia in impeccable Oxford
listing tractor production 1946-49.

Meat. Wheat. Sweaty feet.
Who gets what. The continent

radio sounds, neons, texts,
pools of light around tapedecks

in studios high in the rain dark
of the technicians, the announcers,

voices smooth with such facts
only the sleepless and I hear.

The image remains.

And I think: supposing it's now,
this night the voices all stop.

A flight of wild geese blips the radar
and all the technologies die.

Goodbye Newton Milton Socrates.

And so simple. One man with migraine,
loose signals in Prague,

taxi call signs in Cleveland,
some event in say Valparaiso

or one more demand and no
backout, no manoeuvre, command

begins counting to zero
and beyond into minus,

flips the alert, or a
sleepy technician goes crazy,

falls out with his girlfriend,
slips with his razor

and opens the circuits deep
in the core of the mountains.

This that they're trained for.
This that they're paid for.

This the bullnosed politicians
cadge votes for and all night

the radios sweetly reason around.
This that at age seven

I heard in the long wireless roar
of Hiroshima and prayed

and ran down the garden
sweet God let it not continue.

From Acton to Angel a fireball,
all cities gone:

'An area bounded by Hackney
and Greenwich and Fulham and Willesden,

some millions dead, houses in Bushey
burst into flame.' For weeks

we're told nothing to fret for.
Within 72 hours all programmes

switch to light entertainment,
broken by bulletins.

And the quote ends. Goodbye
radio miracle, Marconi's device.

End of message. Goodbye
to the language that failed.

Goodbye telephone nobody answered.

Goodbye Victorian nude with a ball.
Goodbye all trace on the memory.

Goodbye to everyone in Wimbledon.

Goodbye Fox, my scuttling double
gone in the hot wind of particles.

Goodbye *Areopagitica*, *Aeneid*,
Assyrian Winged Genius, alphabets

running from aleph to zero.
Goodbye Dürer's vision, Blake's angels,

Tolstoy's anger, Shan State,
tears of the Indians, Malleus Maleficorum,

search for the Unified Field Theory,
Fibbonacci Series, Newton's Tables,

Occam's Razor, all gone
in the same sharp withering rain.

Goodbye republics of raw nerve,
disputed borders of meaning.

Goodbye at last, universe
thinking itself in our skulls.

Goodbye love. Woman I loved.

Writing anywhere I said once.
I had just met you. The sharp
intake of breath was mine, the long
unexpected and longed for tide

was you over me. Writing
on stones, on kerbs, on the mucky pavement,
leaving your room at first light
hearing the dawn an outrage of birds.

I write or I die: that dramatic
that simple. I die anyway
while my life is the fool that persists
and is never in his folly any wiser.

A daft occupation some say.
Swinging my lamp whether it's Thursday
or Spain. Somewhere in this
sector of infinite distance I met you,

grey lady who gave me my fox name,
dark lady who gave me my fox shape,
rose lady who gave me my fox colour,
my long fox outline, my fox tongue.

As to *goodbye* not much
to be said for it.
                    I survive
in some core of you
you through my life are the gift of.

One eye shut on the dream
one eye open

One eye hunted
one eye hunter

Aloof alert out
moving abruptly
between skylines

Afloat adrift on the city
some images on the retina

Awake

Fox writes:

once upon a long time
I was a good dog.

I ran around town
with the other good dogs.

Buried our bones.
Brought home bacon.

On paynights drank
Bell's whisky with water,

home by the moon
through the late night streets

in a bad baritone singing
what a terrible thing
is a pub with no beer

down the long hill
to the river. I was

such a good dog
such a bad dog
with the other dogs.

Now I'm Fox. I run.
I've left town.

I run & I run.

I come from a broken home
and I broke it.

Don't wait up for me
Blackbird. Your name

was on mine
like a ring. I'm Fox.

I run and run on
down the vanishing landscape.

I've not paid the mortgage,
I've not paid the bank,

stamp tax or insurance,
I'm a blur, I'm a blank

and I'm never going home.
I've cashed my ticket.

And I've thrown my keys
on the railroad tracks.

And I'm gone.

And I'm Fox, running out.

Into holes under leaves across water.

So far on the hill
and no running back to the treeline,
on in the open.

Fox: hidden in landscape,
visible on it. I run
and my sleep is a dream of running.

Between that and waking
I've glimpsed between fern
and heron's wing the old life.

North by south of Isca the river.
Days were longer there. Even I
might have lived there.

Like a dream of childhood,
willows and tall reeds.
Unlikely as the middle ages,

villages before enclosure,
before these towns I run
hunting my crust in.

Where I fade on the tape,
my shadow with the other shadows
one more missing item.

My voice on the phone
dimming out, my voice asking
are these words coming out of my mouth?

among streets and the mornings
and all these stars
is anyone

who at the end hears traffic,
the siren baying them home
on the brackish roads

on the far sides of towns, sodium
and flyway, strange blue light
that flickers on the ambulance?

Otherwise fast
anomalous
a tube train through allotments
one morning out to Heathrow

A man gone down the country
turning out his tube tickets

trailing his names
cancelling accounts
forwarding addresses

chanting underground underwear
windblown Wimbledon

Barbican
Barbie can't

send the Shah back
Shahn't

out of his skull on

learning how to vanish
hanging on the strap
thinking on his feet
covering the distance

listing strange objects
carried on and off trains

overhearing

dollar
dollar half
bunch of flowers

'Who's a big boy then?
Cooked his own supper?
Washed his socks and underpants?'

So she let you down
poor babba
my little patch of sunlight
maybe she was meant to

Clapham Common Sunday
747 hanging in the sky

split vision
caught connections
razor to the throat

152

bloody carnival
Easter in the city

flute sound
cutting through traffic

he dreams of elsewhere

Victoria by Belgravia
travellers' cases
scuffing the snowcem

Kentucky Fried Chicken boxes

adrift among the residences
pied à terre spacious flat
company let tourists only

down past Justin de Blanc
to the Prince of Wales

old men talking about the war

O walking in the gutter
to avoid bad luck
stepping round a ladder
he was flattened by a truck

didn't give a

Radiation
fades your genes

pagan raider

'them breeding like rabbits
with the H bomb and all'

people knowing no one else

the sixties have gone
but the moustache stays

I read the book
you saw the movie

I saw the real one
the Disney version

dick
lick
prick
tongue
NF skins
clock end
ayatollah Thatcher
kiss my willy
if you're reading this
Mildred
we're through

zipping up his fly

today I'm crow
adrift
wingbeat on wingbeat
split vision
across wet slates
lopped plane trees
hated somehow

the rainbird of Finsbury

something in me
always loving
some part of you

honestly it's my round
after all they're only people

if I'd been a woman
I'd have lost my temper

if I'd been a man
I'd have lost my erection

in Ferme Park Rd waiting for a bus
wondering where
in rain, brick, traffic

skies above Islington
blue
burdened by their beauty

blur of trees
events like birds
marking them

by Angel tube
through the crowd
through the traffic
through the flute music

two buskers, a girl
like a dark linnet singing,
her man fingering the air
to music

how she danced to him
her music
played to him
to no one else

through the tunnels
dusty light on service pipes
slid quickly
back of the brain

Urban. Efficient. Articulate. And costly.

'are you going to the circus?'

clowns lions peanuts painted ladies

Oxford Piccadilly Cambridge
split vision
pub of the same name in which

'Honestly it's my round
you've got to be good to yourself
the electric's cut off
we can't pay the rent
double malts all three Henry'

'has he for whom you
left yours now gone?'

he'll never be a buttercup
in God's shining garden

gifts I'd give my enemy:
gnawings at his brain's
thin skirting

a telephone
ringing in his sleeve
he'll never reach

facefull of fingers
decently bunched Jim

Napoleon's bad smell map of Egypt

          '

hanging on the strap

such a vision of the street
as the street may understand

take your chance at the bar
along with everyone, squire

Fox you say your name was?

glancing on the stairs
my double
his double
Edgware Road

motion of his arm

at Paddington among the trains
grown up and riding double-decker buses
all alone

curtain in the wind
woman calling
someone home to supper

night
distant lights
moon riding clouds

glimpsed twice
his double
one who moves like him

gave chase
hot pursuit

around the Circle Line

gone again down the tubes
the black
fast city veins

to Baker Street
to Jubilee
to Neasden

where he died
easily among the skins
razor to his throat
drowning in his blood
all he ever saw was boots
and the boots going in

hunting down the trains
changing quickly

following the signs
following his shoulder

running
where he dies

running to the razor

opening the doors
awash with blood
where he dies again

spring festival
urban version
late century twenty

film events become
moment as it happens
unrecognisable

swift battering
of images
across the retina

my double
dead

my carnage

dead Fox
dead Fox
dead Fox

But I've seen him
between birdlight and Lisson Grove

between lampdark
and the Long Water

I've seen him

his file closed down the dole office
his last account cleared
his black form
filed with his red form
and his last room cleared
and his suitcase
and his girl told
and his wife told

I've seen him
between Camden and Chalk Farm

slow
easy
waiting for a bus
moving with a grace
moving with a certainty
across the city's face

One of our own they say
served his time

Gone Away on all the envelopes

'My brother thinks I'm dead
but my sisters know I'm alive'

Word

I want a word
a beginning word forming in its water bead

I want a word forming fingers of itself
in the belly of all language

I want a word fusing in the first 4 seconds of the bang

I want a word
striding in the air
all the way to the coda
growing up to be a real person
living where the grown-ups live

where each letter is a life
forming into meaning

I want a word with a gull's lift
and easy shadow
I want a word with a bat's inaudible sound
I want a word like a snail
round and round the rim of a glass

I want a word for these days these miles
these trains this distance
the wanderer covers aloof
on the star-glinting rails

Surbiton Norbiton Sanderstead
blue scatter of sparks
smokey embankment flowers
ownerless back lots of flats
Langham Court Riverdale
in Sledhurst and Streatham
and Gipsy Hill sniffing
amongst the paper plates
the Wonderloaf wrapper detritus
in Hammersmith sniffing the amyl
where I lost sight
lost my name lost my number
my ticket

To Morden to Putney to Wandsworth
to Beckenham Junction
to Stockwell to Battersea Park

Where I was anyone anywhere
on hands and knees
who would crawl to the horizon
finding someone to say *yes* to

just another face
just another walking wounded
starry in the city in a dead space
between Archway and Holloway
in the valley of abandoned bedrooms

just another bruised ego
just another fox

stepping out in the cool skinhead wind
into NF occupied country
to Lambeth evicted boarded-up

through Pakkibashers' Court
through Martin Webster Gardens
to Brick Lane to Bethnal Green

dreaming London Fields and Hackney Downs
spaces between other spaces
states or conditions of mind
a man in a yard bouncing a ball
way down Thatcherland

past the closed-down clinic
and the short-staffed school
such a vision of the street
past the road where the bureaucrats live

through Stepney and south of the river
to Camberwell wary in traffic
through which a sharp blast of dub sound
to Brixton wall-eyed beside the Little Bit Ritzy

oh lady she's long way gone now
in the hennaed rainbow of her hair
you your own man now John
step inside a minute

through the city Muggers Lane
Rape Alley
hunting situations vacant and a room

too old or overqualified
or under experienced or plain can't drive

Long ago now in the year zero
under the rule of Fatso
with my companion Alexander the Impecunious
called Knifeback
called Throatcutter
Jack Scratch
who betrayed me
in the middle of my life
back among the schisms and the alleys
of the hostile villagers
and the slow drawing of the map around Africa
slow drawing of the noose
slow sharpening of the knife
back across the foggy moors
among the stonecutters
among the bands of the black-browed
and their beaded women
there he set his watch
to the exact hour of my defeat
that is finished now

If I want to I'll weep without apology
If I want to I'll laugh
I'll sing with who will sing or sing alone
I will be honest with who will be honest with me

I want a word for a voice
trapped in the telephone
heard only by the post office police
listening for keys
dreaming of a key word listening
for drug words women words
bomb words picket words
words like *immigrant conspiracy abortion*

When all he was asking
in his hardly daring voice
was do you have a room
do you have a job
and how to get
from Balham to Clapham

where he's cowboy
grill chef
beerslinger
checker
porter
typist
punch operator
thief

standing at the cashier's window
hearing *oh we've written a book have we?*

Underneath the night sky.
Star. Star. Star.
I would pray were there any God to pray to

I want the word
for the many lives he might have lived
if he'd gotten off anywhere, Moorgate
for instance or Tooting
in a single room or Dagenham
at the end of a lousy marriage
to a woman hissing in her sleep
alongside him. When he cries
in the onrush at Victoria
and his cry comes out of him
into the world I want
what his cry is: sharp

Always on the wrong train anywhere
with the outdated ticket
in the wrong skin with his
long forgotten biography

Rolling up his last tobacco
and it's midday and it's Monday
and time to feel bad
and it signifies nothing
just another person on the line
when he tips down his hat
and sleeps and wakes knowing
he is called *only the protagonist*

Arrived by the wrong train
to the wrong town hears

no she don't live here no more
your kids grown up and gone
heard she married again
your mother died asking for you
where you been and where you now

At the last there were phone calls
from people who didn't exist

Word I want his word
of the dotty professor
of the salesman hating the product
of the sleepy technician
of the jobless
of the fat man in first I want
word uttered in defeat by the captain
of a wandering band of chartered accountants
word of the bad architects
the government of tax lawyers
all the little stockholders
voting protection in a free economy

166

turning back the clock
deciding what the country needs
is a damned good war

I want word of the tramp on Kingston bridge
dreaming only a warm mug of tea

I want word of the bloke
who leans over with a razor
and slits the protagonist's throat
and walks off scot free

Just another of my feints
Just another invention
Just another of my lies
Just another skin coming off

Switching trains in the train game
playing games with my name game
middle-aged and seedy in rooms
living with a woman it was said
in Eastbourne by the winter sea

Men I knew years back
when I was young and daft
delivering the News of the World
round Pearson Park. Faces
mentioning defeat saying
bankruptcy desertion failure redundancy
lost bottle. Their light
that had gone or never lit
or they burned now on the lamp oil
of necessity the pure oil
of ageing euphoria the door
held half-shut on privacy
sheet smells dusty odour
out of second-hand couches
rent due smell of woman
glimpsed in the kitchen dark

some other dark pursued
room to room through suburbs
in a slow terminal frenzy
their last dance anywhere
under any glittering ball but they
when they talked had not much to say

Such was Fox

In the technologies of terror
On his road to the terminal ward
On his way to the knife
In a taxi to the hospice
In the corner of the interrogation room
Reaching for his last drink in any bar anywhere
Saying *to hell with everything*
Sleeping it off in some room
his night full of idetic images

Fox drawn to the life to the bone
to the yellowing teeth the bristles
at chin and cheek singing barearse
clap hands here comes Charlie

With his word that was word
of the unmasked betrayer
a beaten man knowing better
and had he his time around
but it's too late now Valparaiso

no such thing as a free lunch
sings the radio
where's this highway go to?

him and his egg sandwich

his suffering was only good for when he had to

like a wheel
like a wheel
that stops turning

smiles in death's little sad face

he speaks
from the lengthening floor
of his blood his conviction
not me not me Jack

he speaks
with his word
from the night's narrow places

with his moment
a man bides his breath for
at the end forbears boastmaking

a wise man holds out
his enemies destroy themselves
he defeats them with words

brother shadow
I greet you, goodbye
go well on your road
leave the way open

he is anyone
naked under his clothes
alone his moment

anyone at all wandering back
from the laundromat late Saturday noon
clearing his throat
speaking again
in the white room
sweeping his hat off and asking
who all belongs to this blood then?

* * *

Spartan communiqué

Over in this sector
in the limitless nowhere
setting the mirrors
facing each other

the face shrunk
to its eyeball
its one act
of looking and looking

we find coming between us
ourselves and our vision
that would otherwise be
to infinity

merely our eyes
only our looking.

From the Vale of White Horse: some news

At some cost
I achieved some detachment.

Finding this distance
here in myself
I first had to cross.

Say I got out of the traffic.
I was no longer even curious.
I said bravely *no more bullshit*.

If I lost sight of myself
on the landscape smokey with towns
that barely matters now.

Nor do the years I marched
in my bright brass buttons
behind the wrong flag.

We're each one of us
separate countries I think,
tricky and wary as states.

And the language fools us,
each in the yammering skull
with our messages fading at the border.

I've no complaint in the silence.
I'm alone at last with the stars.

I'm connected by voices and footprints.
I've one eye on the distant foothills.

My news is as ever:
it will not be the last of me.

Being the third song of Urias

Lives ago, years past generations
perhaps nowhere I dreamed it:
the foggy ploughland of wind
and hoofprints, my father
off in the mist topping beats.

Where I was eight, I knew nothing,
the world a cold winter light
on half a dozen fields, then
all the winking blether of stars.

Before like a fool I began
explaining the key in it lost locked box
adding words to the words to the sum
that never works out.

                    Where I was
distracted again by the lapwing,
the damp morning air of my father's
gregarious plainchant cursing
all that his masters deserved
and had paid for.
                    Sure I was
then for the world's mere being
in the white rime on weeds
among the wet hawthorn berries
at the field's edge darkened by frost,
and none of these damned words to say it.

I began trailing out there in voices,
friends, women, my children,
my father's tetherless anger, some
like him who are dead who are
part of the rain now.

In transit
(from Mari for Mick)

Some place a horse
shines on the field. Some place the ants
trek the foothills of the grass.

Maybe love comes and goes
and maybe comes back, scrap of news
from places we lived.

Or it's too late for everything,
childhood and sunglaze
gone from the river. And this
is a grim little song, sister.

As we fly away from each other,
unrepeatable, ordinary,
years away, miles later
chewing love's bit of bread.

Or we're free. That's
what I wanted, always: to be.

Among the white horses.
Among the fields of yellow kale.

Hunéus the shoemaker

He was content all those years
carving his children from wood.

Two nails banged in for eyes
and you're done he told them.

Twice wed he was, his first
lost in childbed, six
that survived out of infancy.

One son he named *Walk in the Lord*,
another *Go Forth*. Taught them his trade
that they make provision.

Working late, kept by his lamp
to prayer and close study.
Frowning under the lintel.

All his life the same music,
patching and stopping up draughts
through sixty some winters.

So much to ask out loud for.
The dark space in his mind
he called God told him so:

mend, shiver, make do when hungry,
suffer when must but make good.

He was content anyway, at nightfall
hunting the wild birds of the river,
a man in his own space.

Or so we believe. That he died
blameless and lonely I'm sure of.

Operations undertaken at or near the surface

Mornings of long silence. I wake late
to the wind and the grey light
of winter coming. The milk
stands cold and alone on the step.

In my dream you shook your dark hair
and turned from me at last.
I bring in the milk.
Yes you loved me for certain.

I think of you. How at times
the world stopped in your hair
where I cried my cry uselessly.
I pour out the milk in the jug.

You betrayed me, having no choice
apparently. Did what you must.
For love of you I scattered my cries
across England. I make tea.

I make it like everything slower these days,
and consider my lack of compassion
back when the world melted in you.
I pour out the milk.

Now your letters no longer arrive.
Your regrets don't whiten the morning.
Winter does that. And my fury.
I pour it all out. I pour it away.

Shallow dreaming

*'it scrambles time and seasons
if it gets through to you'*
     – Joni Mitchell

Sitting in the bus station
where else mister? tuning the transistor
thinking that lady waiting a good lay.

Wearing his snow white bandage
digital timepiece pentacle and earring
a silver razor blade to the throat.

Later with the wires to his head
coasting the big bird from Seattle
beyond the Aleutians and the Circle

or takes the long shift to Bear Island
waving to the Mig *only kidding man*
dropping down the Murmansk approaches

seeing the sky's edge turning south
fuelwards to the Turkish bases
over patchwork Europe and rest up.

That's one duty man over beer and smoke
later the same day *boy that was close*
shooting pool all the world one rush

through the skull one wing of geese
on the snowy wind of the prairie.
Between us and the stars only stars.

Six miles down only clouds more miles
over their shadows. The plane
in the bare knuckle light of the sun

makes at times a rainbow under itself
and the bright ring of colour goes with you
in the radio silence. *It's a pain chief*

that I can tell you. Nothing for hours
over the Baltic probing the Polish margin
testing the Reds. Times out of mind

I've watched them trying it out –
Ilyushin or Bear or flock of wild birds
homing over such landscapes

that show in my scope still –
the long shores of cold where the ocean
batters its freezing continents

and if grass grows there it is chill
rasping and stiff in the sea-brought winds
at the tops of the world.

There the caribou come in spring.
Their hooves still thrash in the sea's ebb
through the tales of the grandfathers.

All blips now. Data printout
as to latitude and the old ice geometry.
I'd quit but what else? I see

white sky on a white world, cities
stubbed out, ash blown catty corner.
I tell you I'd go on an acid tab singing

glimpsing at last a pattern in the grids
kissing goodbye all the ladies
on the planet's side flying in

sliding under the radar yelling
this is a good day to die brothers
nothing lasts only earth and the mountains.

Old movies

It is long ago in an old
old movie, the print bleached,
the soundtrack scratchy and flat.

The actors wear suits and speak
upper-class British, the workmen
are always cheerful and loyal.

They smoke a lot, poised at windows,
their knuckles folded to their faces.
They are all dead now. Overhead

in the high auditorium since demolished
a moth flits in and out the projector beam.
Lint catches in the corners of the shutter.

A film I saw years away in childhood,
in rainy Ripon in the north of my life
before the world showed me its backside.

At the station he waits 40 minutes.
She never arrives among the steam trains.
They never meet again this side

of the last frame of the last reel
before the movie runs off the sprockets.
They won't drink, sit to table, bear children

or share one grain of wheat
of all the world's wheatfields. Before stars
blink out and all the silence starts

her eyes won't be the last he looks into,
her hands the last he falls through,
his voice won't be the last she hears.

In the grey blur of film the protagonist
smokes one last cigarette, loops the butt
off the platform, claps hat on head

and pitches his bag into the next train out,
a nomad pulling up his tent pegs,
his wanderer's reflection in a whisky glass.

And he has no ticket. In the buffet car
the barman counts his change, he says
they come and go they never say their names.

It is another night of trains, blue light
that fades across the fields, a last crow
on a telephone wire and the movie's over.

Transcription of the crying woman

I was making my sounds
I was making them for everyone
I was walking bird alert in pasture
I was wingbeat labouring the easy air

Did he expect no change in me
who was not one but many?
It took the two of us I told him
the drowning and the drowned

I put on silk I put on lace
I oiled my olive skin
I was the mirror's glance
as I was dressing for my lover

All through these woods I was
beating in the bird hunt
too long I was alone
and he where was he where?

While I was hennaing my hair
while I was in my mirror's silver
while he was numbering the roads
while he was calling up from Maida

I took one lover then another
I was buckling on my purple dress
I was straightening out my seam
I was still dreaming of the south

I was the seal I was gazelle
I went running by the strath
I was tucking in my children
I was sweetening their milk

And I was running for the running
I was the otter's skin
across my lover's skin
I was infinity of cries

I took him in my hands like prayer
I took him in my mouth
I took the wafer of him to my tongue
I sucked the sweetness from him

I took the salt I took the wine
I was his nun I was his whore
I was the gull pitched into wind
I was a song spilled in the beams

My name was being called
my name was *bird on water*
my name was *spent and howling*
my name was *he is butchered*

I was undressing for my lover
I was pronouncing all my words for him
my shoe my clasp o my sweet moth
I was unravelling my tongue

When I was fiddling with my button
when I was picking out my comb
when I was lacquering my nails
his death came beating on my air

I was whirling in the thicket
I was thrashing in the sea foam
I was running in the scrubland
I was falling down the mountain

I was calling for my mother
I was dressing for my lovers
I was calling to my children
I was crackling in my satin

I was staring at his death's head
I was remembering his hands
I was encountering his blood
I was alone forever then

I was all Ivan's seven wives
I was Sobakina meaning *canine*
I was Nogaya meaning *naked*
I was the fury in the light across my flesh

Planting aloes
(for Judi)

Days of random events,
waking with no plan,
all the city mine to play in.

And whatever else I do
I'll be no damned richer
by the evening. *Can't dance*

too wet to plough.
Cut myself shaving.
Unsnarled the white kitchen.

Emptied out the trash.
Filled little red pots
with dark London soil,

planting the aloes
my mother gave me hours ago
yesterday in Yorkshire.

So come live with us
little green-sleeves.
Like the throats of birds.

A slow careful work
that's repetitive,
my mind drifting off

hanging in the moment
I'm tucking roots
among muck's spaces.

Sounds of far traffic,
blackbird, woman's nextdoor voice
and rattle of a bowl.

Dog's yap. April light
warm across my shoulder.
I am awake again, my life

suddenly its centre.
You I love
who taught me aloes heal.

Red blossom through the suburbs.
Yellow blaze forsythia makes.
Skies forever changing.

Words forming into meaning.
Take the aloes. Take from me
of all my pages, this love.

Mouth

Mouth of a soft shell
I put my ear to hear the sea in you

Sighting eye of the sextant
I put my own eye to read the constellations
where are no stars no starcharts

Mercury
mirror without glass
scoop
sickle
shoe of the first step in Pavlova's dance
telephone to the sea's deep
I put my mouth to hear the word in you
I touch you with my tongue it is a prayer

Sibilant
first mark first ideogram
first aleph for all alphabets
first futhark of the script of pagan raiders
first winter count of zero zero zero
a language made of vowels only
words spoken into water

Like a day of leaves in rainy wind
like the tongues of shoes
like the first plants come ashore
like a cabinet of drawers and secrets
like the flickered pages of a book
like the spaniel's ears
like the flaps of aviators' helmets
like the lips of horses
like the petals of magnolia flickering pink, white
like the blue of burning anis
and the strange translucent brown
beneath the rose skin
where your blood is hunting for the surfaces of light

Like the fish mouth risen into air
like the moon's reflection stretched on water

A chanterelle
a cedar chest
a cupboard stocked against a coming war
a cave of smuggled liquor
ogival arch where no madonna is
a box of soft cutlery
the flower's throat going back in you
far into the centre of all liquids

Where was my terror
where my joy is
where my anger is
where my fear of the dark we come from
and the dark we go into is

Like a bird through a byre of the Saxons
like the swan's road on water
like the first stages on the long journey into Russia
like the tracks of fish
like the keel's shuck into waves' trough

The long afternote of a bell
the anemone
sifting all the sea through its marrying ring

Tongue

My tongue is a flute
filling all the tunnels of the subway
with its flute sound

My tongue goes before me
My tongue says my tongue
in the chatter of my quiet

184

No more a singer than the reeds
my tongue's a bird sound
a throstle
singing in the tree of memory

My tongue's a busker
much interested in loose change
but my tongue plays anyway

My tongue has no stops
My tongue has no reed
as a flute has none

My tongue goes rolling into words
My tongue goes running into language
My tongue goes rifling the alphabets
hunting through vocabularies
saying *honey ant   palanquin   labial*

My tongue unlocks my word hoard
My tongue says I'm a fool to let it speak

My tongue is all the fortune that I have
for any of my children

My tongue's a daft errand boy
running on ahead
My tongue's an old messenger
forgetting what he came for

Telling women that I love them
Saying that I'll stay
Promising *I'll pay I'll pay I'll pay*

And when my tongue gets me shot
my tongue will ask for one last cigarette
compliment the squaddies on their turnout
order *ready aim fire*
and quote Lorca
to the gunfire
I'll never hear

The Ubi Sunt variations

1

I shall account some lost things:
twelve songs for a missing flute.
I have lost even their titles:

> *He returns from the frontier*
> *He finds his house deserted*
> *She writes from far away*
> *He despairs beside the river*

2

In some lost book I recall
in a photograph taken Brighton Beach,
Lee Miller, Paul Éluard, Eileen Agar, 1936.

The seawind blows in their faces.
They sit in deckchairs in the sunlight
of the moment that contains them,
gone the road of all moments.

3

Bones no bigger than a child's
that were the warrior's, the fierce
man-killing frame of him

mineral again, climbing the bog-cotton,
rounding the sheep's horn,
singing down the flute singing
in the love of you I lost myself.

4

In the long lost weekend of my life
we gathered herbs she and I
with the full white moon in Orion.

And all night crushed and blended,
mortared, pestled, pinched
finger to thumb and scattered.
But who knows what that meant now?

5

They lied about the heart:
that it's a soft pink cushion
sitting in the left wall of the chest.

A lie I outlived. Time passed
in the study of linoleum in basement rooms,
an old slow war that fought itself
over the long slope of my life.

6

In trunks packed in haste,
randomly, my lost books, notes,
photographs, lost again as they must be.

The wanderer resumes his journey.
Makes do with what's to hand.
The air fills with banal words:
how I love you, we'll meet again.

7

And each night in the dream's house
the hand was a hand waving *help*.
Say I ran, say I was hunted

ditch after ditch, life after life,
a creature that slept by water
and woke among cities, strangered
and half way human. Say that.

8

Traveller on the old road
of the wind between towns,
say I endured.

Singing *short of nowt we've got.*
Singing *not much but we eat it all.*
Singing *clap hands for Charlie.*
Singing *love this is my country.*

9

In the capital as in the provinces:
disaffection and less work, scattered riots,
the imperial currency worth less and less.

Rebellion seethes in the suburbs.
The governors strengthen the police.
Dark clouds, no rain yet from the west.
The ugly prince marries the virgin.

10

Set the fire up. Let there be drink
for these travellers. There was a time
once my brothers I was young

and what lay till now ahead
was mist along a river, the kestrel
in sunlight hung his moment
over the tall reed beds running south.

11

Dear mother father aunt Jessie
it is no picnic, it's France I think
there's no white tablecloths.

We're all that thinks in all the stars,
inventing telephones and missiles.
Then silence from the planet.
Nothing more. The hiss of radiation.

12

Hills blued with distance.
No goodbye. A little further
we begin to see the mountains.

And the river's small beginnings.
And the sea turning its only syllable.
And the nights where no one sleeps.
And the song that is the last.

The poet reclining
after Chagall

What still holds me,
where I stretch in my skin
at the day's edge:

a particular landscape,
the fence at the field's side,
what my hat keeps the rain from.

The moment, once and once only,
sufficient, taken on trust
in the wheels of the watch.

The wind stirs the foxgrass.
The lapwing enters the thicket.

Where had the world gone?

Did I invent it,
making a fiction to keep off sleep
for fear I'd dream worse?

So I devised the grass
and the raggety birch bark,
the spider's morning extrusions
beaded white with the mist.

So it was. When I snapped my fingers,
when I turned, when I opened my eyes,
when I clapped my hands and called out,
my voice came back empty.

The morning, the evening.
Everything vanishes, generations
fading into the grass.

I lay down. I counted
the words she had written
in barbed High Gothic script:

behind wire I can't live.
The wind took her words off.
I lay down without sleeping.

Mine always the want
to make more of what is,
the world from its nothings:

the assemblies of grass,
fallen leaf ticking pavestone,
water drop forming and falling.

Out of sight were old gates
swinging in wind, far hiss
of a highway of traffic.

Further off smokey towns
with their townsmen's scandals.
City glitter of gossip and money.

In the streets coffee smells
and newly baked bread.
I met train after train

but her train never arrived.
I wrote *kleine Mutti*
so far you can't walk
to the wire you can see it.

I should forget such a place ever was.
I should concern myself with the city,
living there and surviving.

That's enough. I should forget my thought
the best's gone and the rest gets darker.

But for my belief
in the grass, that it is once
and once it is
it is forever.

I hear it all still: sheep's bleat on the moor
and the peewee's thin calls in the weeds.

The geese: I hear their cry in traffic,
the gate's squeal in brakes,
in the high thunder of the planes overhead
the wind gunning through the pines.

Long ago. A psychiatrist
told me not to listen to the wind
but the wind tells me not to listen to him.

I'll be the one holding the forged winning ticket.
I'll be the one with the devalued currency.
I'll be at the airport with no flight anywhere.
I'll be on the quayside in the bombed-out harbour
deciding once again to abandon my luggage.
I'll be in the right and I'll be dead wrong again.

Let this be the scald of remembered country.
Here the river turns east.
Here the geese fly over my grandfather's house.

Soldiers march off between trees
into the dark elbow of the road's curve.

The gate's lost its sneck.
Tiles rain from the barn roof.
Trees break in the gale, lightning divides some.

There will be sleet, then long winter.

There is a dotted line dividing the house from itself.
In the general's office this district is maps.
In the war college the cowshed an objective.
There is a red pin where the pig's snout roots.
Tank radios chatter in the fir trees.
There is a bullet-hole where the horse crops.
Here the rockets fall and the fallout
obliterates the grass and the old field divisions.

He lies in the paddock.
It is mid summer.
Not a leaf has yet fallen
but the sky changes towards day's end.

He dreams the dark evergreen,
the resins in the calendars of wood.

Waking, the byre and the brown horse
will again surprise him.

The night music

Long notes of a late instrument
drawn out across the balconies.

The stairwells newly painted.
The windows open for the night air.

By day small cage birds
hung over steep streets
dropping thin weepy notes.

The sadness of the bars.
Their air that's thickened with hashish.

By night there is the distance
like a blanket and the heavy air,
a man's breath pared along a reed
played late and to no purpose.

Across the streets in moonlight
the music fading off into a nowhere
made of dark and dog yelps
battling for the suburbs. It is
another night, another country
in another lost city where I scribbled
if I die leave the way open.

All my years one bullet
travelled from the mined-out minerals
through assembly lines until it found me.
At the end I never saw it.
So goodbye my heart, my name.

That was long ago,
a life that was or would be.
It finished somewhere halfway.

Moment by moment it sheds
more of itself. I move away
in a new name with a new biography.

This is the next world already.

Everything shines much as before.

Nothing has changed, even I.

Fox in October

He forgave the grass its persistence.
He forgave the sky its blue indifference,
no longer angry with the high wintry cirrus.

Horizon to horizon across prairies,
oceans, towns and villages the planet
spun day in day out through sunlight
into dark again, century by century
of rainy violence what was the sky
but a great yawn
wherever he was on the Earth
in any of its histories,
small in all his armour.

He forgave it. Were there a god
among the rafts of stars
he must be bored by now or had to be joking.

His eye to Herschel's telescope,
his ear to the radio noise
out at the last edge of the little we know,
in the dark of the planetarium
or in the pavilion at Kew
staring up into the points of light
he saw himself.

He was merely a protagonist,
his bag of words across his shoulder.
He forgave that.

He forgave the brown leaves.
He forgave the pigeons their dullness.
He forgave childhood its passing.
He forgave the left side of his brain.

He forgave his enemies.
He forgave his friends.
He forgave himself.
He forgave his betrayals.
He survived his own foolishness.
Some he'd damaged he hoped survived him.

Wind clattered the dropped leaves
across the afternoon park,
the long sunlight guttered,
blackbird with traffic.

He forgave his mother her growing older,
wiser, braver. He forgave
his father his death after decades of meaningless fury,
a flint pitched at the sheer injustice
of his bosses. And everyone else.

It was hard on the Earth.
He forgave everyone that.
Some that had almost broken him
he supposed he'd forgive. He did not forgive
in the name of anyone else nor the years
spent wasted and gone asking
were some evil or just daft,
either way meaning the same word *trouble*.

He forgave his children
miles years stars falling away
since his abandoning them.
He forgave their forgiving him, loving him.
He forgave even her.

He forgave love its almost ruining him.
He forgave its illusion.
He forgave himself that.

In a mood to forgive all,
make his peace, live his life now
with the woman he loved who loved him
without need of forgiveness.

Those we properly love travel with us
some way down time in the distance
the stars scatter their light
particle by particle forming new dust,
new tides in new galaxies,
perhaps for no reason.

They don't give up.
However many tries it takes.
However many lives it takes.

He concluded, one day in October,
at the beginning of an early winter,
sunlight sheer between the plane trees
at Crouch End, in his cold northern country.

* * *

Bibliography

The Poet Reclining includes all the poetry which Ken Smith wants to keep in print from books and pamphlets published between 1962 and 1980. It also includes poems from *Grainy pictures of the rain*, published in America in 1981, as well as some recent uncollected poems. The selection does not cover two recent Bloodaxe titles, *Burned Books* (1981) and *Abel Baker* (1982). While some prose pieces appear as parts of sequences, the selection does not draw upon Ken Smith's prose books; these are marked in the list below with a dagger †. A selection of Ken Smith's prose pieces will be published by Bloodaxe Books in 1983.

After the complete list of Ken Smith's publications, the poems included in *The Poet Reclining* are listed under each title. Poems which have appeared in more than one book are marked with an asterisk*.

Eleven Poems (Northern House, 1964)
The Pity (Jonathan Cape, 1967)
Academic Board Poems (Peeks Press, 1968)
Arc Pamphlets 4 & 5 (Arc Publications, 1969)
Work, distances/poems (Swallow Press, Chicago, 1972)
The Wild Rose † (Stinktree Press, Memphis, 1973)
Hawk Wolf (Sceptre Press, 1974)
Frontwards in a backwards movie † (Arc Publications, 1975)
Wasichi (Aloes Books/Spanner, 1975)
Anus Mundi † (Four Zoas Press, Mass., 1976)
Island called Henry the Navigator † (Cat's Pajamas, Ill., 1976)
Tristan Crazy (Bloodaxe, 1978)
Tales of the Hunter (Night House, Boston, 1979)
the joined-up writing † (X Press, 1980)
What I'm Doing Now (Oasis Books, 1980)
Fox Running (Rolling Moss Press, 1980; Bloodaxe, 1981)
Between the Dancers (Circle Press, 1980)
Grainy pictures of the rain (Truedog Press, Arkansas, 1981)
Burned Books (Bloodaxe, 1981)
Abel Baker Charlie Delta Epic Sonnets (Bloodaxe, 1982)

Eleven Poems
Family group*; Grass*; The pity*.

The Pity
Family group*; The street; Country: Keld to Reeth; Grass*; The pity*; The hunter; Water; A fragment.

Academic Board Poems
The boss*.

Arc Pamphlets 4 & 5
The child's version*; The son; Gravedigger; Bitter*.

Work, distances/poems
Exiles; Dream journeys; She speaks; The child's version*;
The boss*; Bitter*; Where winter begins; In Pennsylvania,
winter's end; After a journey; Little Notes; Persistent narrative;
Crying woman; Song for the whites; From the Nahua; The
Sioux cleared from Minnesota; Ghost songs; Ghost dances;
Where did I learn such quiet [as *Untitled*]. *THE WILD TURKEY*
[as *CALLING THE WILD TURKEY*]: Wild Turkey One; Wild
Turkey Two; Living in the Danelaw [as *The Danelaw*];
Another part of his childhood; A description of the lichway;
Wild Turkey Six; A farewell to the city of Exeter; In the
Americas, so the tale goes; The author, a teacher of petomania;
A journey through part of western Pennsylvania. THE ELI
POEMS [as *THE DEAD ORCHESTRA*]: The marsh; The third
month; Eli's poem; The rooming house; His lament; The
obsession; What was done.

Hawk Wolf
Wolf vision; Hawk vision.

Wasichi
Valley*; The clearing.

Tristan Crazy
One for sorrow; Two for nobody; Three: tales of the hunter*;
Four, being a prayer to the western wind*; Five, which is
here by the river; Six: the wife's complaint; Seven: when he
can't sleep for thinking; Eight. The singer; Nine: Shorty's
advice to the players*; Ten: the tale unfinished*.

Tales of the Hunter
Tales of Urias the shape-shifter; Old postcards of the river;
The Swan; Reports from the east; From the southern river;
At the western beacon, the second of the songs of Urias [as
Among the dancers, being the second of the songs of Urias]; TRISTAN
CRAZY three [as *Tales of the Hunter*]*, four [as *The fourth song
of Urias, a prayer to the western wind*]*, nine [as *Shorty's advice to
the players*]*, and ten [as *The message*]*.

What I'm Doing Now

Playing field observations; Caesar Caesar; A right curse on the enemy; Spartan communiqué; From the vale of White Horse; Being the third song of Urias [as 'Lives ago . . .']; In transit; Hunéus the shoemaker; Operations undertaken at or near the surface; Transcription of the crying woman; Planting aloes; Mouth; Tongue.

Fox Running

This has been revised and extended.

Between the Dancers

Moiré effect*.

Grainy pictures of the rain

My father fading out; Valley*; Childhood in the lowlands; Sunk Island, that winter; The Tivoli Bar; Federico; Maria the thief; The veterans; Peasant; Duck at Haldon Ponds; Moiré effect*.

Uncollected poems

Acknowledgements are due to the editors of the following magazines and anthologies in which the following uncollected poems have appeared: *Boston Phoenix* for 'Remembering when he was a wolf'; *London Magazine* for 'Old business: the drowned bride'; *New Poems 1972-73*, edited by Douglas Dunn (P.E.N./ Hutchinson, 1973) for 'To survive'; *Not Poetry* for 'Six items heard in three locations', 'At the collège des beaux arts', and 'Some unfinished movements'; *Perfect Bound* for the 'Fun City Winter' sequence; *Poems for Shakespeare 4*, edited by Anthony Rudolf (Globe House Publications, 1976) for 'Winter occasions'; *Seizure* (Eugene, Oregon) for 'Half songs, 1790'; *Stand* for 'To survive', 'Bowl', 'Wants', 'Fly', and 'Lake'; *Surviving in America* (Tucson, Arizona) for 'The door'; *Telegram* for 'The poet reclining' and 'The night music'; and *23 Modern British Poets*, edited by John Matthias (Swallow Press, Chicago, 1971), also published as issue 21 of *Triquarterly* (Evanston, Ill.), for 'The stone poems'.

The following poems are previously unpublished: 'Another night of muttering'; 'Crocus'; 'Surprised again beside the river'; 'Shallow dreaming'; 'Old movies'; 'the Ubi Sunt variations'; 'Fox in October'.

Index of Titles and First Lines

Ken Smith was born in 1938 in Yorkshire. He has taught, edited, worked as a barman, a reader for the BBC, and as a freelance writer. His work has appeared in numerous magazines and anthologies in Britain and America.

From 1969 to 1973 Ken Smith lived in the USA. In 1972-73 he was Visiting Writer for Clark University and Holy Cross, Massachusetts; in 1976-78 the Yorkshire Arts Fellow in Creative Writing at Leeds University; and in 1979-81 Writer in Residence at Kingston Polytechnic. He is a former editor of *Stand* and *South West Review*. He now lives in London.

Paul Stangroom was born in 1955 in Washington, Co. Durham. He studied Fine Art at the Central School of Art and Design, London, and at Sunderland Polytechnic. His drawings and paintings have been widely exhibited, and he has worked with poets on several publications. Some of his drawings for poems by Frances Horovitz were included in *Wall* (LYC Gallery, 1981), and their collection of poems and drawings, *Snowlight, Waterlight*, will appear from Bloodaxe in 1983. He lives in Newcastle.